A BOOK
OF LIVING POEMS

A BOOK OF
LIVING POEMS

Compiled and
Edited by

WILLIAM R. BOWLIN

A LAIRD & LEE PUBLICATION

ALBERT WHITMAN & COMPANY

CHICAGO ILLINOIS

1946

ACKNOWLEDGMENTS

Copyright material in this book is used by permission of and by special arrangement with: Houghton Mifflin Company for *The Ghostly Galley* and *My Wage*, by Jessie B. Rittenhouse, *The Boys* by Oliver Wendell Holmes, *Nature* and *The Old Clock on the Stairs*, by Henry W. Longfellow, *Aladdin*, by James Russell Lowell; Harper & Brothers, for *The Homeland*, by Dana Burnet; Charles Scribner's Sons, for *By an Open Window in Church*, by Corinne Roosevelt Robinson, *The Zest of Life*, by Henry van Dyke; E. P. Dutton & Co. for *The Spires of Oxford*, by Winifred M. Letts; Douglas Malloch for *You Have to Believe*; Charlotte P. Gilman for *The Lion Path* and *I Resolve*; Nancy Byrd Turner for *Good Night*; Mrs. Clinton Scollard for *The Great Voice, Dusk*, and *If Only the Dreams Abide*, by Clinton Scollard; Theodosia Garrison Faulks for *One Fight More* and *The Dreamers*; Angela Morgan for *A Song of Life*; Cale Young Rice for *The Mystic*; Farrar & Rinehart, Inc., for *Tears*, by Lisette Woodworth Reese; Dodd Mead & Co. for *Over the Shoulders and Slopes of the Dune*, by Bliss Carman; Mrs. Buel P. Colton for *Keep Thou My Heart*, by Buel P. Colton; Elizabeth Virginia Raplee for *Nostalgia*; Miriam Teichner for *Awareness, The Struggle*, and *Victory*; Ruth Messenger for *A Fear*; Samuel Ellsworth Kiser for *A Little Prayer* and *It May Be*; Mavis Clare Barnett, for *Silence*; Amelia Earhart for *Courage*; Mr. A. L. Felkin for *The Wisdom of Folly*, by Ellen Thornycroft Fowler; Edith Thomas Howe for "Frost Tonight," and *If Still They Live*, by Edith M. Thomas; Margaret Larkin for *Good-by—To My Mother*; Ernest McGaffey for *I Fear No Power a Woman Wields*; Elsie Janis for *My Prayer*; Grace Denio Litchfield for *To a Hurt Child*; Victor Starbuck for *The Dead*; Frederic F. Van de Water for *The Last Tourney*; Virginia Lyne Tunstall for *They Sleep So Quietly*.

FOREWORD

Following the kindly reception of the first volume, *A Book of Treasured Poems,* it seemed desirable to call this volume *A Book of Inspirational Poems.* It was so called in manuscript. But on reflection the publishers and editor decided against the adjective "inspirational," chiefly because the word has developed a misleading connotation. Inspirational poetry has come to be associated with rimed advice, with the frenzied urge to hold on, to fight, to die if necessary for one's ideas, without considering whether it were wise to hold on or whether the ideas are worth dying for.

Inspirational poetry should draw from a spring much deeper than mere determination. Inspiration rises far back in great causes, in the eternal verities, in our own individual allocations in life.

In general, it may be said that much so-called inspirational writing is verse rather than poetry. No one has ever satisfactorily defined poetry. We do not always know when a poem is great and we never know why it is so. Perhaps a poem is great when it is a kind of window that lets us see more deeply beyond commonplace things; or because, like great music, it identifies us inwardly in the time-enduring fabric of perfect things.

Poems are living because they have gained residence in the life-pattern of a people. Many in this volume have long held such place, and the editor believes many more need but to be known to become a part of ourselves—living poems.

—*William R. Bowlin*

C·O·N·T·E·N·T·S

PAGE

Building the Bridge for Him—*Miss W. A. Dromgoole*........ 13
Over the Shoulders and Slopes of the Dune—*Bliss Carman*.... 14
Fortune's Finger—*William Shakspere* 14
Take Heart—*Edna Dean Proctor*......................... 15
I Teach School—*Anonymous*............................. 16
Keep Thou My Heart—*Buel P. Colton*.................... 17
Light Within—*John Milton*............................. 17
Self-Dependence—*Matthew Arnold* 18
Cares—*Elizabeth Barrett Browning*...................... 19
As Toilsome I Wandered—*Walt Whitman*.................. 20
Flower in the Crannied Wall—*Alfred Tennyson*............ 21
No Enemies—*Charles Mackay*........................... 21
As in Silks My Julia Goes—*Robert Herrick*................ 22
Delight in Disorder—*Robert Herrick*..................... 22
By an Open Window in Church—*Corinne Roosevelt Robinson*. 23
Nostalgia—*Elizabeth Virginia Raplee*..................... 24
"Frost Tonight"—*Edith M. Thomas*....................... 25
Creation—*Ambrose Bierce* 25
Sonnet on His Blindness—*John Milton*.................... 26
My Creed—*Howard Arnold Walter*....................... 26
Lullaby—*Alice Herbert* 27
Poise—*Violet Alleyn Storey*............................. 27
Say Not the Struggle Nought Availeth—*Arthur Hugh Clough*.. 28
A Little While I Fain Would Linger Yet—*Paul Hamilton
    Hayne* 29
He's Just—Away—*James Whitcomb Riley*.................. 30
So Live—*William Cullen Bryant*......................... 31
Spinning—*Helen Hunt Jackson*.......................... 32
The Boys—*Oliver Wendell Holmes*....................... 33
Let Me Live Out My Years—*John G. Neihardt*.............. 35

Vice—*Alexander Pope* 35

A Noiseless, Patient Spider—*Walt Whitman*................. 36

Borrowing Trouble—*Robert Burns*......................... 36

Remember Now—*Bible* 37

Byron—*Cincinnatus Hiner (Joaquin) Miller*............... 38

My Task—*Robert Louis Stevenson*......................... 39

Victory—*Miriam Teichner* 39

Bruce to His Men at Bannockburn—*Robert Burns*............ 40

Good-By—To My Mother—*Margaret Larkin*............... 41

German Prisoners—*Joseph Johnston Lee*................... 42

Inscription—*Sir William Watson*......................... 42

Prospice—*Robert Browning* 43

Home—*Hermann Ford Martin*............................. 44

Myself—*Anonymous* 45

Why Should a Man—*William Shakspere*................... 45

The Brave at Home—*Thomas Buchanan Read*............... 46

One Woman—*Zoë Akins*................................... 47

Silence—*Mavis Clare Barnett*............................. 48

The Second Coming—*Norman Gale*....................... 48

Epistle to a Young Friend—*Robert Burns*................. 49

The Wanderer—*Eugene Field*............................. 52

A Hero—*Florence Earle Coates*........................... 53

The World's Needs—*Ella Wheeler Wilcox*................. 53

The Spires of Oxford—*Winifred M. Letts*.................. 54

Opportunity—*Walter Malone* 55

Tears—*Lizette Woodworth Reese*......................... 56

Uneasy Lies the Head—*William Shakspere*............... 57

If Still They Live—*Edith M. Thomas*..................... 58

The Last Tourney—*Frederic F. Van de Water*.............. 59

The Mystic—*Cale Young Rice*............................ 60

The Parting Guest—*James Whitcomb Riley*................ 62

To James Whitcomb Riley—*Bide Dudley*.................. 62

The Two Friends—*Charles Godfrey Leland*................ 63

The Zest of Life—*Henry van Dyke*........................ 64

Auld Daddy Darkness—*James Ferguson*................... 65

The Bars of Fate—*Ellen M. H. Gates*..................... 66

I Resolve—*Charlotte Perkins Gilman*..................... 67

The Old Clock on the Stairs—*Henry Wadsworth Longfellow*... 68

One Fight More—*Theodosia Garrison*..................... 70

Death I Can Understand—*Anonymous*...................... 71

Immortal Craftsmen—*Daniel Webster*.................... 71

I Am the Door—*Anonymous*............................. 72

Cowards—*William Shakspere* 72

En Garde, Messieurs—*William Lindsay*.................. 73

Tomorrow and Tomorrow—*William Shakspere*............. 74

Plays—*Walter Savage Landor*........................... 74

Called Back—*Emily Dickinson*.......................... 75

New Every Morning—*Susan Coolidge*.................... 76

Sonnet on Chillon—*Lord Byron*......................... 77

The Dead—*Victor Starbuck*............................. 78

Company—*Richard R. Kirk*............................. 78

Gradatim—*J. G. Holland*............................... 79

A Little Prayer—*Samuel Ellsworth Kiser*................. 80

To a Hurt Child—*Grace Denio Litchfield*................ 81

Thrice Armed—*William Shakspere*...................... 81

So Be My Passing—*William Ernest Henley*............... 82

Ozymandias of Egypt—*Percy Bysshe Shelley*............. 83

Words—*Alexander Pope* 83

If This Were Faith—*Robert Louis Stevenson*.............. 84

The Rose and the Gardener—*Austin Dobson*.............. 85

I Will Lift Up Mine Eyes—*Bible*....................... 86

Sin Is Sin—*Anonymous*................................ 86

The Wisdom of Folly—*Ellen Thornycroft Fowler*........... 87

At the Crossroads—*Richard Hovey*...................... 88

Standards—*Charles Wharton Stork*...................... 89

The Sands of Dee—*Charles Kingsley* 90

Scythe Song—*Andrew Lang*............................. 91

From His First Song—*Robert Burns*..................... 91

The Bell Buoy—*Rudyard Kipling*....................... 92

My Daily Creed—*Anonymous*........................... 94

I Fear No Power a Woman Wields—*Ernest McGaffey*........ 95

Solitude—*William Allingham* 95

The Great Voice—*Clinton Scollard*...................... 96

It May Be—*Samuel Ellsworth Kiser*..................... 96

A Fear—*Ruth Messenger*............................... 97

America the Beautiful—*Katherine Lee Bates*.............. 98

Three Gates—*From the Arabian*......................... 99

Happiness—*Katherine Beeman* 100

Per Aspera—*Florence Earle Coates*...................... 100

Nearer Home—*Phoebe Cary*............................ 101

Courage—*Amelia Earhart* 102

The Bell—*James Rorty*................................. 103

The Greatness of the Soul—*Alfred Tennyson*............... 104

Life—*Edward Rowland Sill*............................. 105

Dusk—*Clinton Scollard* 105

From Ulyssus—*Alfred Tennyson*......................... 106

The Trumpeter—*Thomas Wentworth Higginson*............. 107

The Ghostly Galley—*Jessie B. Rittenhouse*................. 107

A Song of Life—*Angela Morgan*......................... 108

"I Shall Not Make a Garment of My Grief"—*Roselle Mercier Montgomery* 109

The Homeland—*Dana Burnet*........................... 110

Playing the Game—*Anonymous*......................... 110

Interlude—*Ella Wheeler Wilcox*......................... 111

A Rhyme for Thanksgiving—*Edwin Markham*.............. 112

Windy Nights—*Robert Louis Stevenson*................... 113

A Ballad of Heroes—*Austin Dobson*..................... 114

Mors Benefica—*Edmund Clarence Stedman*................ 115

The Lion Path—*Charlotte Perkins Gilman*................. 116

In a Public Library—*Alethea Todd Alderson*............... 117

The Eternal Goodness—*John Greenleaf Whittier*............ 118

My Prayer—*Elsie Janis*................................ 120

Good Deeds—*William Shakspere*........................ 120

They Sleep So Quietly—*Virginia Lyne Tunstall*............. 121

The Trailing Arbutus—*John Greenleaf Whittier*............ 122

My Wage—*Jessie B. Rittenhouse*........................ 123

The Struggle—*Miriam Teichner*......................... 123

Nature—*Henry Wadsworth Longfellow*................... 124

Love Slumbers On—*Percy Bysshe Shelley*................. 125

Sometimes—*Thomas S. Jones, Jr.*....................... 125

He Whom a Dream Hath Possessed—*Sheamus O'Sheel*...... 126

You Have to Believe—*Douglas Malloch*................... 127

A Farewell—*Charles Kingsley*.......................... 128

Up-Hill—*Christina Rossetti* 128

The Goal—*Ella Wheeler Wilcox*........................ 129

If Only the Dreams Abide—*Clinton Scollard*.............. 130

Sonnet—*William Wordsworth* 131

Awareness—*Miriam Teichner* 132
The Freeman's Creed—*Anonymous*....................... 132
Good Night—*Nancy Byrd Turner*........................ 133
By Bendemeer's Stream—*Thomas Moore*.................. 134
But Once—*Anonymous* 134
The Round Trip—*McLandburgh Wilson*.................. 135
The Human Touch—*Richard Burton*..................... 135
The Sailor Boy—*Alfred Tennyson*....................... 136
Pictures of Memory—*Alice Cary*........................ 137
When the Kye Comes Hame—*James Hogg*................. 138
Morality—*Matthew Arnold* 140
The Prose-Poetry of Lincoln—*Abraham Lincoln*........... 141
Why?—*Anonymous* 142
The Mountain Girl—*DuBose Heyward*.................... 143
Irony—*Mabel Wing Castle*............................. 144
The Dreamers—*Theodosia Garrison*..................... 145
A Thought to Remember—*Robert Louis Stevenson*......... 145
Aladdin—*James Russell Lowell*......................... 146
A Spark o' Nature's Fire—*Robert Burns*................. 146
The Patter of the Rain—*Coates Kinney*................. 147
Intimations of Immortality—*William Wordsworth*.......... 148

A BOOK
OF LIVING POEMS

Keep your face al—
ways turned toward
the sunshine and
the shadows will
fall behind you.

BUILDING THE BRIDGE FOR HIM

W. A. Dromgoole

Miss Dromgoole, American newspaper woman, has dramatized the spring of human progress in her simple poem, Building the Bridge for Him. Science, invention, education—all are building bridges for "him."

An old man, traveling a lone highway,
Came at the evening cold and gray,
To a chasm deep and wide.

The old man crossed in the twilight dim,
For the sullen stream held no fears for him.
But he turned when he reached the other side,
And builded a bridge to span the tide.

"Old man," cried a fellow pilgrim near,
"You are wasting your strength with building here;
Your journey will end with the ending day,
And you never again will pass this way.

"You have crossed the chasm deep and wide.
Why build you a bridge at eventide?"
And the builder raised his old gray head:
"Good friend, on the path I have come," he said,
"There followeth after me today
A youth whose feet will pass this way.

"This stream, which has been as naught to me,
To that fair-haired boy may a pitfall be;
He, too, must cross in the twilight dim—
Good friend, I am building this bridge for him."

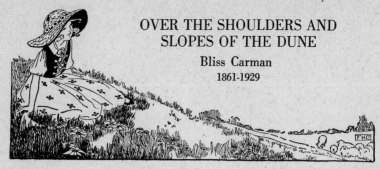

OVER THE SHOULDERS AND SLOPES OF THE DUNE

Bliss Carman
1861-1929

Bliss Carman, Canadian by birth, first came into literary prominence when he and Richard Hovey wrote the Songs of Vagabondia. His are songs of the open road, the sea, autumn—freedom, not so much nationally as personally and spiritually. Carman's first book, Low Tide on Grand Pré was immediately successful because it presaged a new art in poetry.

Those who are fortunate enough to have seen the march of flowers across the dunes, especially in the dunes of Northern Indiana, must recognize the picture.

> Over the shoulders and slopes of the dune
>   I saw the white daisies go down to the sea,
> A host in the sunshine, an army in June,
>   The people God sends us to set our hearts free.
>
> The bobolinks rallied them up from the dell,
>   The orioles whistled them out of the wood,
> And all of their singing was "Earth it is well,"
>   And all of their dancing was "Life, thou art good."

FORTUNE'S FINGER

William Shakspere
1564-1616

From Hamlet, Act 3, Sc. 2, L. 77.

>   . . . . .and blest are those
> Whose blood and judgment are so well commingled,
> That they are not a pipe for Fortune's finger
> To sound what stop she please. Give me that man
> That is not passion's slave, and I will wear him
> In my heart's core, ay, in my heart of heart,
> As I do thee.

TAKE HEART

Edna Dean Proctor

1838-1923

Edna Dean Proctor's home was in Massachusetts "where sea winds pierce the solitudes." The storm breaks on the shore but the poet looks beyond the dark and rainy sea to where the bluebird waits for April skies.

All day the stormy wind has blown
    From off the dark and rainy sea;
No bird has past the window flown,
The only song has been the moan
    The wind made in the willow tree.

This is the summer's burial-time:
    She died when dropped the earliest leaves;
And, cold upon her rosy prime,
Fell direful autumn's frosty rime;
    Yet I am not as one that grieves,—

For well I know o'er sunny seas
    The bluebird waits for April skies;
And at the roots of forest trees
The May-flowers sleep in fragrant ease,
    The violets hide their azure eyes.

O thou, by winds of grief o'erblown,
    Beside some golden summer's bier,—
Take heart! Thy birds are only flown,
Thy blossoms sleeping, tearful sown,
    To greet thee in the immortal year!

When I am forgotten, as I shall be,
And sleep in dull cold marble,

* * * * *

Say, I taught thee.
—*Henry VIII, Act III, Sc. 2, L. 433*

I write no poem men's hearts to thrill,
No song I sing to lift men's souls;
To battle front, no soldiers lead;
In halls of state I boast no skill;
I just teach school.

I just teach school. But poet's thrill,
And singer's joy, and soldier's fire,
And stateman's power—all—all are mine;
For in this little group where still
I just teach school

Are poets, soldiers, statesmen—all:
I see them in the speaking eye,
In face aglow with purpose strong,
In straightened bodies, tense and tall,
When I teach school.

And they, uplifted, gaze intent
On cherished heights they soon shall reach.
And mine the hands that led them on!
And I inspired—therefore content,
I still teach school.

KEEP THOU MY HEART

Buel P. Colton
1852-1906

*Professor Colton was for years a teacher in the Illinois
State Normal School at Normal, Illinois. When, after his
death in 1906, this little poem came to light among his
effects in his mountain cabin, the hundreds who had shared
his love of the great outdoors stood silent, feeling that somewhere Nature keeps the heart of those who love her.*

Keep thou my heart till summer comes again,
O little cabin folded in God's hills.
Here in the city's toil it has small part;
I cannot make it happy. Care and pain
Will be its portion where the myriad ills
Of life surround it. Take my tired heart
Safe in the promise of a thousand springs,
Where it can hide away and take its rest.
The snow will comfort it; the April rain
Will waken it with all the growing things
That slumber in the dear Earth-Mother's breast.
Keep thou my heart till summer comes again.

LIGHT WITHIN

John Milton
1608-1674

*Conscience warns us as a friend before it punishes us as a judge.—
Stanislaus.*

He that has light within his own clear breast
May sit i' the center, and enjoy bright day:
But he that hides a dark soul and foul thoughts
Benighted walks under the midday sun;
Himself in his own dungeon.

SELF-DEPENDENCE

Matthew Arnold
1822-1888

*The poetry of Matthew Arnold is restrained
and dignified, but for all its sweet austerity,
moving and inspirational. A "resolve to be thyself," unruffled by either fear or doubt—that
is Matthew Arnold.*

Weary of myself, and sick of asking
  What I am, and what I ought to be,
At this vessel's prow I stand, which bears me
  Forwards, forwards, o'er the starlit sea.

And a look of passionate desire
  O'er the sea and to the stars I send:
"Ye who from my childhood up have calm'd me,
  Calm me, ah, compose me to the end!

"Ah, once more," I cried, "ye stars, ye waters,
  On my heart your mighty charm renew;
Still, still let me, as I gaze upon you,
  Feel my soul becoming vast like you!"

From the intense, clear, star-sown vault of heaven,
  Over the lit sea's unquiet way,
In the rustling night-air came the answer:
  "Wouldst thou *be* as these are? *Live* as they.

"Unaffrighted by the silence round them,
  Undistressed by the sights they see,
These demand not that the things without them
  Yield them love, amusement, sympathy.

"And with joy the stars perform their shining,
  And the sea its long moon-silver'd roll;
For self-poised they live, nor pine with noting
  All the fever of some differing soul.

"Bounded by themselves, and unregardful
    In what state God's other works may be,
In their own tasks all their powers pouring,
    These attain the mighty life you see."

O air-born voice! long since, severely clear,
    A cry like thine in mine own heart I hear:
"Resolve to be thyself; and know, that he
    Who finds himself, loses his misery!"

CARES

Elizabeth Barrett Browning

1806-1861

Elizabeth Barrett was for many years an invalid, living in a darkened room. Finally she met Robert Browning, and her love for him gave her the strength to elope with him in 1846. Theirs was a singularly beautiful romance and the fifteen years of life remaining to her were full of happiness.

The little cares that fretted me,
    I lost them yesterday
Among the fields above the sea,
    Among the winds at play;
Among the lowing of the herds,
    The rustling of the trees,
Among the singing of the birds,
    The humming of the bees.

The foolish fears of what may happen,
    I cast them all away
Among the clover-scented grass,
    Among the new-mown hay;
Among the husking of the corn
    Where drowsy poppies nod,
Where ill thoughts die and good are born,
    Out in the fields with God.

CARES is sometimes credited to Louise Imogen Guiney. The authorship is in doubt.

AS TOILSOME I WANDERED

Walt Whitman

1819-1892

Whitman was an ideal more than a poet. He was the voice of a hunger— a hunger to be free and honest in literary things. He supplanted the nice, well-turned objective word and phrase and theme with the real name, the direct phrase, and the commonplace, subjective thought. He was first in poetry to call a spade a spade and prove that such calling could be a poem. While he has been overrated as a poet, and while much of his poetry is too formless to last, it must be remembered that we straighten a crooked stick by bending it too far the other way.

As toilsome I wander'd Virginia's woods,
To the music of rustling leaves, kick'd by my feet, (for 'twas
    autumn),
I mark'd at the foot of a tree the grave of a soldier;
Mortally wounded he and buried on the retreat (easily all could I
    understand),
The halt of a mid-day hour, when up! no time to lose—yet this
    sign left,
On a tablet scrawl'd and nail'd on the tree by the grave,
Bold, cautious, true, and my loving comrade!

Long, long I muse, then on my way go wandering,
Many a changeful season to follow, and many a scene of life,
Yet at times through changeful season and scene, abrupt, alone, or
    in the crowded street,
Comes before me the unknown soldier's grave—comes the inscrip-
    tion rude in Virginia's woods,
Bold, cautious, true, and my loving comrade.

FLOWER IN THE CRANNIED WALL

Alfred Tennyson
1809-1892

There is something in the nature of things which the mind of man, which reason, which human power cannot effect, and certainly that which produces this must be better than man. What can this be but God?—Marcus Tullius Cicero, C. 70 B. C.

It was in 1870 A. D. that Tennyson wrote these six lines.

Flower in the crannied wall,
I pluck you out of the crannies,
I hold you here, root and all, in my hand,
Little flower—but *if* I could understand
What you are, root and all, and all in all,
I should know what God and man is.

NO ENEMIES

Charles Mackay
1814-1889

In order to have an enemy one must be somebody.—Swetchine.

You have no enemies, you say?
Alas, my friend, the boast is poor;
He who has mingled in the fray
Of duty, that the brave endure,
Must have made foes! If you have none,
Small is the work that you have done.
You've hit no traitor on the hip,
You've dashed no cup from perjured lip,
You've never turned the wrong to right,
You've been a coward in the fight.

AS IN SILKS MY
JULIA GOES

Robert Herrick
1591-1674

Herrick was of the Cavalier poets, "worldly idle, clever, gay, and a clergy-man of the church of England. He had a country parish in the West. In the pulpit he preached (at least we hope so) Christian virtues, and in his verse he pleasantly encouraged young and old to get along happily without them, at least while life and health lasted. . . At its best his verse expresses with wonderful beauty the innocent joys of life, the freshness of English Maytime, the lightness of youth, the sense of being young and gay in the open sunshine."*

When as in silks my Julia goes
Then, then, methinks, how sweetly flows
The liquefaction of her clothes!

Next, when I cast my eyes and see
That brave vibration each way free,
—O how that glittering taketh me.

 # DELIGHT IN DISORDER
Robert Herrick
1591-1674

A sweet disorder in the dress
Kindles in clothes a wantonness:
A lawn about the shoulders thrown
Into a fine distraction:
An erring lace, which here and there
Enthralls the crimson stomacher:
A cuff neglectful, and thereby

*English Literature, Herbert Bates.

Ribbands to flow confusedly:
A winning wave, deserving note
In the tempestuous petticoat:
A careless shoe-string, in whose tie
I see a wild civility:
Do more bewitch me than when art
Is too precise in every part.

BY AN OPEN WINDOW
IN CHURCH

Corinne Roosevelt Robinson

1861-1932

A rich sense of perfect rest—itself the perfect end of all our hours.
Mrs. Robinson was a sister of the late Theodore Roosevelt.

I hear the music of the murmuring breeze,
It mingles with the preacher's quiet word;
Dim, holy memories are waked and stirred,
I seem to touch once more my mother's knees.
Christ's human love, His spirit mysteries
Envelop me. It is as though I heard
An angel choir in the singing bird
That floats above the fair full-foliaged trees.
The old sweet Faith is singing in my breast
With peace in Nature's summer subtly blent,
All my being breathes a deep content—
Life and its unremitting, baffled quest
Fade into this rich sense of perfect rest—
My soul, renewed, is steeped in sacrament.

NOSTALGIA

Elizabeth Virginia Raplee

Nostalgia—homesickness. God made the country and man made the town.

The calm shade shall bring a kindred calm and the sweet breeze that makes the green leaves dance shall waft a balm to thy sick heart.

—Bryant

My eyes are tired of brick, of steel and stone,
My ears are weary with the noise of crowds.
   A longing fills me just to be alone
Where there are only trees, and grass, and clouds.
The city chokes me with its heedless rush;
Its ruthless buildings reaching toward the sky
Stifle my dreams; I want to feel the hush
    Of evening, and to watch a lone bird fly
    Into the sunset. Just to know again
The hills and meadows of my former days;
To hear the patter of the Summer rain;
To wander idly where a brooklet strays.

What has the city to compare with these?—
Where else the peace, and where the strength I find
    In the benign companionship of trees?
    Here is a solace for the tired mind
Not all the city's varied attributes
    Can offer. Let me feel again the spell
Which in my inmost being strikes its roots—
    The magic of the land I loved so well.

"FROST TONIGHT"
Edith M. Thomas
1854-1925

Miss Thomas, whose delicate strength of verse has gained her the heart of a wide public, is said to have taken her great inspiration from the encouragement of Helen Hunt Jackson whom she met in 1881.

Apple-green west and an orange bar,
And the crystal eye of a lone, one star . . .
And, "Child, take the shears and cut what you will,
Frost tonight—so clear and dead-still."

Then, I sally forth, half sad, half proud,
And I come to the velvet, imperial crowd,
The wine-red, the gold, the crimson, the pied,
The dahlias that reign by the garden-side.

The dahlias I might not touch till tonight!
A gleam of the shears in the fading light,
And I gathered them all—the splendid throng,
And in one great sheaf I bore them along.

*   *   *   *   *

In my garden of Life with its all-late flowers,
I heed a Voice in the shrinking hours:
"Frost tonight—so clear and dead-still" . . .
Half sad, half proud, my arms I fill.

CREATION
Ambrose Bierce
1842-1913

And God said, Let there be Light.—Bible.

God dreamed—the suns sprang flaming into place,
And sailing worlds with many a venturous race.
He woke—His smile alone illumined space.

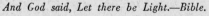

SONNET ON HIS BLINDNESS

John Milton

1608-1674

The fame of Milton is always associated with his now unremembered Paradise Lost but generally most appreciated in his immortal "They also serve who only stand and wait."

When I consider how my light is spent
　　Ere half my days, in this dark world and wide,
　　And that one talent, which is death to hide,
Lodged with me useless, though my soul more bent
To serve therewith my Maker, and present
　　My true account, lest He returning, chide:
　　"Doth God exact day labor, light denied?"
I fondly ask; but Patience, to prevent
　　That murmur, soon replies, "God doth not need
　　Either man's work, or His own gifts; who best
　　Bear His mild yoke, they serve Him best.
　　　　His state
Is kingly. Thousands at His bidding speed,
　　And post o'er land and ocean without rest;
　　They also serve who only stand and wait."

 # MY CREED
Howard Arnold Walter

A creed above creeds—above religions, or races. This excellent poem has been set to music.

I would be true, for there are those who trust me;
　　I would be pure, for there are those who care;
I would be strong, for there is much to suffer;
　　I would be brave, for there is much to dare.

I would be friend of all—the foe, the friendless;
    I would be giving and forget the gift;
I would be humble, for I know my weakness;
    I would look up—and laugh—and love—and lift.

LULLABY
Alice Herbert

Critics have called this the loveliest lullaby in the language.

Sleep soft and long, no morn is worth the waking.
The world has tears for waking eyes to weep.
Beat soft and strong, dear heart too small for breaking.
    Little one, gentle one, sleep!

Out in the rain lies one who will not waken,
Out in the night lies one whose dreams are deep;
What can it mean to you, the word "forsaken"?
    Little one, laughing one, sleep!

POISE
Violet Alleyn Storey

You will end life just as you close a favorite book,
    Turn off the shaded light and slowly climb the stairs.
With you there'll be no startled cry, no wondering look
    When you behold the Room you've entered unawares.

SAY NOT THE STRUGGLE
NOUGHT AVAILETH

Arthur Hugh Clough

1819-1861

Clough, son of a Liverpool merchant, wandered widely—to America, back to teach in the great universities of England, back again to the home of nine-teenth century poets, Cambridge, in Massachusetts; then on to Italy where he died suddenly of fever. Say Not is his chief right to literary memory.

Say not the struggle nought availeth,
    The labor and the wounds are vain,
The enemy faints not, nor faileth,
    And as things have been they remain.

If hopes were dupes, fears may be liars;
    It may be, in yon smoke conceal'd,
Your comrades chase e'en now the fliers,
    And, but for you, possess the field.

For while the tired waves, vainly breaking,
    Seem here no painful inch to gain,
Far back, through creeks and inlets making,
    Comes silent, flooding in, the main.

And not by eastern windows only,
    When daylight comes, comes in the light,
In front, the sun climbs slow, how slowly,
    But westward, look, the land is bright.

A LITTLE WHILE I FAIN WOULD LINGER YET

Paul Hamilton Hayne

1830-1886

The lines of this excellent poem are heightened by the courage of the man. Representative of the distinguished family that gave Senator Hayne to South Carolina, Colonel Hayne entered the Civil War and served the Confederate cause until hardship and ill health drove him back to his ruined home where he waged a courageous fight against ill health and poverty.

A little while (my life is almost set!)
   I fain would pause along the downward way,
   Musing an hour in this sad sunset-ray,
While, Sweet! our eyes with tender tears are wet:
A little hour I fain would linger yet.

A little while I fain would linger yet,
   All for love's sake, for love that cannot tire;
   Though fervid youth be dead, with youth's desire,
And hope has faded to a vain regret,
A little while I fain would linger yet.

A little while I fain would linger here:
   Behold! who knows what strange, mysterious bars
   'Twixt souls that love, may rise in other stars?
Nor can love deem the face of death is fair:
A little while I fain would linger here.

A little while I yearn to hold thee fast,
   Hand locked in hand, and loyal heart to heart;
   (O pitying Christ! those woeful words, "We part!")
So ere the darkness fall, the light be past,
A little while I fain would hold thee fast.

A little while, when light and twilight meet,—
   Behind, our broken years; before, the deep
   Weird wonder of the last unfathomed sleep,—
A little while I still would clasp thee, Sweet,
A little while, when night and twilight meet.

A little while I fain would linger here;
　　Behold! who knows what soul-dividing bars
　　Earth's faithful loves may part in other stars?
Nor can love deem the face of death is fair:
A little while I fain would linger here.

HE'S JUST—AWAY*

James Whitcomb Riley

1849-1916

Riley's humor was the more effective because it was always kindly, even tender. When on July 22, 1916, Riley himself went—just away, the world might well have applied his poem to its author.

I cannot say, and I will not say
That he is dead.—He is just away!

With a cheery smile and a wave of the hand,
He has wandered into an unknown land,

And left us dreaming how very fair
It needs must be, since he lingers there.

And you—O you, who the wildest yearn
For the old-time step and the glad return,—

Think of him faring on, as dear
In the love of There as the love of Here;

And loyal still, as he gave the blows
Of his warrior-strength to his country's foes.—

Mild and gentle, as he was brave,—
When the sweetest love of his life he gave

To simple things:—Where the violets grew
Pure as the eyes they were likened to,

The touches of his hands have strayed
As reverently as his lips have prayed:

When the little brown thrush that harshly chirred
Was dear to him as the mocking-bird;

And he pitied as much as a man in pain
A writhing honey-bee wet with rain.

Think of him still as the same, I say:
He is not dead—he is just—away!

SO LIVE

William Cullen Bryant

1794-1878

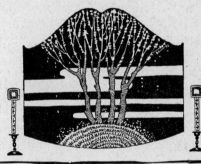

From Thanatopsis written when Bryant was but nineteen.

So live that when thy summons comes to join
The innumerable caravan that moves
To that mysterious realm, where each shall take
His chamber in the silent halls of death,
Thou go not, like the quarry-slave at night,
Scourged to his dungeon, but, sustained and soothed
By an unfaltering trust, approach thy grave
Like one who wraps the drapery of his couch
About him, and lies down to pleasant dreams.

SPINNING
Helen Hunt Jackson
1831-1885

Helen Hunt Jackson has attained immortality in the great novel Ramona, written in 1884. She and Emily Dickinson were born in Amherst, Mass., within a year of each other, but their paths led far apart.

She was always tender and sincere in her work. Her grave in the mountains of Colorado is the scene of many pilgrimages, and upon it is a pyramid of stones cast there as tribute by those who love her memory.

Like a blind spinner in the sun,
    I tread my days;
I know that all the threads will run
    Appointed ways;
I know each day will bring its task,
And, being blind, no more I ask.

I do not know the use or name
    Of that I spin:
I only know that some one came,
    And laid within
My hand the thread, and said, "Since you
Are blind, but one thing you can do."

Sometimes the threads so rough and fast
    And tangled fly,
I know wild storms are sweeping past,
    And fear that I
Shall fall; but dare not try to find
A safer place, since I am blind.

I know not why, but I am sure
    That tint and place,

In some great fabric to endure
    Past time and race,
My threads will have; so from the first,
Though blind, I never felt accurst.

But listen, listen, day by day,
    To hear their tread
Who bear the finished web away,
    And cut the thread,
And bring God's message in the sun,
"Thou poor blind spinner, work is done."

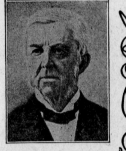

THE BOYS

Oliver Wendell Holmes

1809-1894

This poem was written for the reunion of the Class of Harvard, 1829, held January 6, 1859. The "boy" whom Fate tried to conceal under the name of Smith was Samuel Francis Smith, author of America.

Has there any old fellow got mixed with the boys?
If there has, take him out, without making a noise.
Hang the Almanac's cheat and the Catalogue's spite!
Old Time is a liar! We're twenty to-night!

We're twenty! We're twenty! Who says we are more?
He's tipsy—young jackanapes—show him the door!
"Gray temples at twenty?"—Yes! *white* if we please;
Where the snow-flakes fall thickest there's nothing can freeze!

Was it snowing I spoke of? Excuse the mistake!
Look close—you will see not a sign of a flake;
We want some new garlands for those we have shed —
And these are white roses in place of the red!

We've a trick, we young fellows, you may have been told,
Of talking (in public) as if we were old:
That boy we call "Doctor," and this we call "Judge";
It's a neat little fiction—of course it's all fudge.

That fellow's the "Speaker"—the one on the right;
"Mr. Mayor," my young one, how are you to-night?
That's our "Member of Congress," we say when we chaff;
There's the "Reverend" What's-his-name?—don't make me laugh.

That boy with the grave mathematical look
Made believe he had written a wonderful book,
And the Royal Society thought it was *true!*
So they chose him right in; a good joke it was, too!

There's a boy, we pretend, with a three-decker brain,
That could harness a team with a logical chain;
When he spoke for our manhood in syllabled fire,
We called him "The Justice," but now he's "The Squire."

And there's a nice youngster of excellent pith:
Fate tried to conceal him by naming him Smith;
But he shouted a song for the brave and the free—
Just read on his medal, "My country," "of thee!"

You hear that boy laughing? You think he's all fun;
But the angels laugh, too, at the good he has done.
The children laugh loud as they troop to his call,
And the poor man that knows him laughs loudest of all!

Yes, we're boys—always playing with tongue or with pen;
And I sometimes have asked, Shall we ever be men?
Shall we always be youthful and laughing and gay,
Till the last dear companion drops smiling away?

Then here's to our boyhood, its gold and its gray!
The stars of its winter, the dews of its May!
And when we have done with our life-lasting toys,
Dear Father, take care of thy children, The Boys!

LET ME LIVE OUT MY YEARS*
John G. Neihardt
1881-

John Gneisenau Neihardt, by act of the legislature, poet laureate of the state of Nebraska, is noted for the masculine strength that marks his poetry. He is literary editor of the St. Louis-Post-Dispatch.

Let me live out my years in heat of blood!
Let me die drunken with the dreamer's wine!
Let me not see this soul-house built of mud
Go toppling to the dust—a vacant shrine!

Let me go quickly like a candle light
Snuffed out just at the heyday of its glow.
Give me high noon—and let it then be night!
Thus would I go.

And grant me when I face the grisly Thing,
One haughty cry to pierce the gray Perhaps.
O let me be a tune-swept fiddlestring
That feels the Master-Melody—*and snaps!*

 ## VICE
Alexander Pope
1688-1744

One sin doth provoke another.—Shakspere.

Vice is a monster of so frightful mien,
As to be hated, needs but to be seen;
Yet seen too oft, familiar with her face,
We first endure, then pity, then embrace.

*From *Collected Poems*, John G. Neihardt. By permission of The Macmillan Company.

A NOISELESS PATIENT
SPIDER

Walt Whitman

1819-1892

Whitman and his poetry were often assailed in his day as immodest—and even immoral. How blind is the Present! How antipodal may be fact and judgment! Whitman was the modern literary Diogenes seeking the honest poet who should dare to face unvarnished life with honesty,—seeking truth till the gossamer thread catch somewhere.

A noiseless, patient spider,
I mark'd where, on a little promontory, it stood isolated;
Mark'd how, to explore the vacant vast surrounding,
It launched forth filament, filament, plament, out of itself,
Ever unreeling them—ever tirelessly speeding them.

And you O my Soul where you stand,
Surrounded, detached, in measureless oceans of space,
Ceaselessly musing, venturing, throwing, seeking the spheres to con‹
    nect them,
Till the bridge you will need be form'd, till the ductile anchor hold;
Till the gossamer thread you fling, catch somewhere O my Soul.

 ## BORROWING TROUBLE

Robert Burns

1759-1796

If men lost their troubles they'd hunt for them.—Avery.

But human bodies are sic fools,
For a' their colleges an' schools,
That when nae real ills perplex them,
They mak enow themsels to vex them;
An' ay the less they hae to sturt them,
In like proportion less will hurt them.

REMEMBER NOW

The Bible

Ecclesiastes, XII, 1-14

Year after year in the bookstalls of the world the one best seller is the Bible. One reason for its perennial appeal is the grandeur of its ancient Hebrew poetry.

Remember now thy Creator in the days of thy youth:

    Or ever the evil days come,
And the years draw nigh
      When thou shalt say, I have no pleasure in them:

    Or ever the sun,
      And the light,
      And the moon,
      And the stars,
Be darkened,
And clouds return after the rain:

In the day when the keepers of the house shall tremble,
And the strong men shall bow themselves,
And the grinders cease because they are few,
And those that look out of the windows be darkened,
And the doors shall be shut in the street;

When the sound of the grinding is low,
And one shall rise up at the voice of a bird,
And all the daughters of music shall be brought low;
Yea, they shall be afraid of that which is high,
And terrors shall be in the way;

And the almond tree shall blossom,
And the grasshopper shall be a burden,
And desire shall fail:

Because man goeth to his long home,
And the mourners go about the streets:

Or ever the silver cord be loosed,
Or the golden bowl be broken,
Or the pitcher be broken at the fountain,
Or the wheel broken at the cistern:

And the dust return to the earth,
    As it was;
And the spirit return unto God
    Who gave it.

BYRON

Joaquin Miller

1841-1913

Those who prefer to wallow in the grayish details of the mortal side of our famous men in preference to reveling in their genius might do well to consider the point of view of the sage Joaquin Miller.

In men whom men condemn as ill
I find so much of goodness still,
In men whom men pronounce divine
I find so much of sin and blot,
I do not dare to draw a line
Between the two, where God has not.

MY TASK

Robert Louis Stevenson
1850-1894

Stevenson was the most loved literary man of his age. He was physically weak and had been so from childhood. We are touched by his lament about having to go to bed while other children played. Yet few men have presented to life so great an example of calm, wise courage. He lived his Task.

To be honest, to be kind;
To earn a little and to spend a little less;
To make upon the whole a family happier for his presence;
To renounce when that shall be necessary and
    not to be embittered;
To keep a few friends, but those without capitulation,—
Above all, on the same grim conditions, to keep
    friends with himself—
Here is a task for all that a man has of
    fortitude and delicacy.

VICTORY

Miriam Teichner
1888-

What is defeat? Nothing but education.—Wendell Phillips.

I call no fight a losing fight
If, fighting, I have gained some straight new strength;
If, fighting, I turned ever toward the light,
All unallied with forces of the night;
If, beaten, quivering, I could say at length:
"I did no deed that needs to be unnamed;
I fought—and lost—and I am unashamed."

BRUCE TO HIS MEN AT BANNOCKBURN

Robert Burns

1759-1796

Of these stirring patriotic lines Burns wrote to a friend: "There is a tradition, which I have met with in many parts of Scotland, that it (the air Hey, tuttie taitie) was Robert Bruce's march at the battle of Bannockburn. This thought, in my yesternight's evening walk, warmed me to a pitch of enthusiasm on the theme of liberty and independence, which I threw into a kind of Scottish ode, fitted to the air, that one might suppose to be the gallant Royal Scot's address to his heroic followers on that eventful morning."

That eventful morning was June 24, 1314. Thirty thousand English under their king Edward II met Robert Bruce and his Scots across the Bannock, a little burn to the south of Sterling Castle, and were disastrously overthrown. Scots, Wha Hae is the national air of Scotland.

> Scots, wha hae wi' Wallace bled,
> Scots, wham Bruce has aften led,
>   Welcome to your gory bed,
>   Or to victory!
>
> Now's the day, and now's the hour;
> See the front o' battle lour;
> See approach proud Edward's power—
>   Chains and slavery!
>
> Wha will be a traitor knave?
> Wha can fill a coward's grave?
> Wha sae base as be a slave?
>   Let him turn and flee!

Wha for Scotland's king and law
Freedom's sword will strongly draw,
Freeman stand, or freeman fa',
    Let him follow me!

By oppression's woes and pains!
By your sons in servile chains!
We will drain our dearest veins,
    But they shall be free!

Lay the proud usurpers low!
Tyrants fall in every foe!
Liberty's in every blow!—
    Let us do or die!

GOOD-BY—TO MY MOTHER

Margaret Larkin

This lovely lyric won first prize from the Kansas Author's Club when it appeared in 1921 in the Kansas City Star.

Let not your heart be altogether lonely
Now that the last reluctant words are said,
I take away my face and voice, but leave you
My heart, instead.

Our separate lives will only make love dearer,
And beautiful as distant mountains are,
When all the little hills erase each other,
And leave no scar.

For every westward-blowing wind is my wind,
Dawning I send you, when my sun is high,
And all God's lovely stars are ours together.
Good-by! Good-by!

GERMAN PRISONERS

Joseph Johnston Lee

Joseph Lee, Englishman, was a sergeant in the 4th Battalion of the famous Black Watch regiment of the British Army during the Great War. German Prisoners is from his Ballads of Battle. He himself became a prisoner in Germany.

When first I saw you in the curious street
Like some platoon of soldier ghosts in grey,
My mad impulse was all to smite and slay,
To spit upon you—tread you 'neath my feet.
But when I saw how each sad soul did greet
My gaze with no sign of defiant frown,
How from tired eyes looked spirits broken down,
How each face showed the pale flag of defeat,
And doubt, despair, and disillusionment,
And how were grievous wounds on many a head,
And on your garb red-faced was other red;
And how you stooped as men whose strength was spent,
I knew that we had suffered each as other,
And could have grasped your hand and cried, "My brother!"

INSCRIPTION

On a rock resembling the human face

Sir William Watson

1858-

The sea-fowls build in wrinkles on my face.
Ages ere man was, man was mocked by me.
Kings fall, gods die, worlds crash; at my throne's base
In showers of bright white thunder breaks the sea.

[42]

PROSPICE

Robert Browning

1812-1889

Robert Browning was the husband of Elizabeth Barrett Browning. Prospice—looking forward—and now we look backward at his passing and know he feared not.

Fear death?—to feel the fog in my throat,
    The mist in my face,
When the snows begin, and the blasts denote
    I am nearing the place,
The power of the night, the press of the storm,
    The post of the foe;
Where he stands, the Arch Fear in a visible form,
    Yet the strong man must go:
For the journey is done and the summit attained,
    And the barriers fall,
Though a battle's to fight ere the guerdon be gained,
    The reward of it all.
I was ever a fighter, so—one fight more,
    The best and the last!
I would hate that death bandaged my eyes, and forbore,
    And bade me creep past.
No! let me taste the whole of it, fare like my peers
    The heroes of old,
Bear the brunt, in a minute pay glad life's arrears
    Of pain, darkness and cold.
For sudden the worst turns the best to the brave,
    The black minute's at end,
And the elements' rage, the fiend-voices that rave,
    Shall dwindle, shall blend,
Shall change, shall become first a peace out of pain,
    Then a light, then thy breast,
O thou soul of my soul! I shall clasp thee again,
    And with God be the rest!

HOME
Hermann Ford Martin

The poem Home was published in The Fugitive, March, 1923. It is one of the best of its decade.

He left his office for the street,
    Glad that the night at last had come,
Eager to rest his tired feet,
    And be with her at home.

He felt that he was growing old.
    His dreams were now of bread and meat
That once were filled with beauty's gold,
    And the wild sea and sweet.

And came into his mind the day
    He had left ship, and sea, and tide,
That he might not be long away
    From his slim-bodied bride.

Then, musing still, with wistful eyes,
    Alone, he stepped into the night,
And there beneath those starless skies
    Met the consuming light.

*   *   *   *   *

He did not know that he was dead,
    But somehow felt that he was free,
And, from the road that homeward led,
    He turned towards the sea.

MYSELF
Anonymous

The reverence of a man's self is, next to religion, the chiefest bridle of all vices.—Bacon— New Atlantis.

I have to live with myself, and so
I want to be fit for myself to know;
Always to look myself straight in the eye.
I don't want to stand, with the setting sun
And hate myself for the things I've done.
I want to go out with my head erect;
I want to deserve all men's respect;
But here in the struggle for fame and pelf
I want to be able to like myself.
I don't want to look at myself and know
That I'm bluster and bluff and empty-show.
I never can fool myself; and so,
Whatever happens, I want to be
Self-respecting and conscience-free.

 ## WHY SHOULD A MAN—
William Shakspere
1564-1616
From the Merchant of Venice.

Let me play the fool:
With mirth and laughter let old wrinkles come,
And let my liver rather heat with wine
Than my heart cool with mortifying groans.
Why should a man whose blood is warm within
Sit like his grandsire cut in alabaster?
Sleep when he wakes, and creep into a jaundice
By being peevish?

THE BRAVE AT HOME

Thomas Buchanan Read
1822-1872

*This little poem belongs unquestionably in McGuffy's readers. But it is
a mistake to abandon a good piece of literature simply because it is in an
outworn mode. It states a truth and it undoubtedly belongs in the list of
poems destined to be remembered.*

Read's vocation was portrait painting but on his poem rests his fame.

The maid who binds her warrior's sash
    With smile that well her pain dissembles,
The while beneath her drooping lash
    One starry teardrop hangs and trembles,
Though Heaven alone records the tear,
    And fame shall never know her story,—
Her heart has shed a drop as dear
    As e'er bedewed the field of glory!

The wife who girds her husband's sword
    'Mid little ones who weep and wonder
And bravely speaks the cheering word,
    What though her heart be rent asunder,
Doomed nightly in her dreams to hear
    The bolts of death around him rattle,—
Hath shed as sacred blood as e'er
    Was poured upon the field of battle!

The mother who conceals her grief
    While to her breast her son she presses,
Then breathes a few brave words and brief,
    Kissing the patriot brow she blesses.

With no one but her secret God
　　To know the pain that weighs upon her,—
Sheds holy blood as e'er the sod
　　Received on Freedom's field of honor!

ONE WOMAN

Zoë Akins

1886-

And Abraham rose up early in the morning, and took bread and a bottle of water, and gave it unto Hagar, putting it on her shoulder, and her child, and sent her away; and she departed and wandered in the wilderness of Beersheba.—Gen. 21:14.

Mercy more becomes a magisrate than the vindictive wrath which men call justice.—Longfellow.

Since I heard them speak of her great shame
　　I looked upon her face with curious eyes,
　　But pity in my heart became surprise,—
Finding not any havoc there, nor flame;
Only a little smile that went and came,
　　As if she knew a mirth too great and wise
　　And far too proud to serve the world with lies,
Disdaining as she did its praise or blame.

She who had passed through sin, as through a door,
　　Stayed not upon the steps to wail and beat
Against a portal closed for evermore:
　　But smiled, and went her way with tireless feet,
　　When night had passed and the long day begun;—
So Hagar faced the desert with her son.

SILENCE
Mavis Clare Barnett

The silence of the place was like a sleep, so full of rest it seemed.—
Longfellow.

God must have loved the silence for He laid
   A stillness on the sunset and the dawn;
     Upon the moment when the bird has gone,
Leaving a note, high-hung, within the glade,
More sweet than when he sang it; noons that pass
   Too full of forest changelessness for sound;
   Creeping of little frosts along the ground;
Silence of growth among the summer grass.

God must have deeply loved the silences,
   For is there one of us who has not heard
     Promptings to silence that he speaks not of?
What of an old remorse; a hope that is
   Too deeply hoped; what of a grief out-grown;
     And silent, old, unconquerable love?

 ## THE SECOND COMING
Norman Gale
1862-

The Savior came. With trembling lips
He counted Europe's battleships.
"Yet millions lack their daily bread:
So much for Calvary!" He said.

EPISTLE TO A YOUNG FRIEND

Robert Burns

1759-1796

The Epistle to a Young Friend was written in May, 1786, ten years before Burns' untimely death. It was addressed to Andrew Aiken, son of Robert Aiken, to whom Burns had inscribed his immortal The Cotter's Saturday Night.

Excepting only Shakspere, the noblest name in English poesy is Robert Burns.

I lang hae thought, my youthfu' friend,
    A something to have sent you,
Though it should serve nae ither end
    Than just a kind memento;
But how the subject-theme may gang,
    Let time and chance determine;
Perhaps it may turn out a sang,
    Perhaps turn out a sermon.

Ye'll try the world fu' soon, my lad,
    And, Andrew dear, believe me,
Ye'll find mankind an unco squad,
    And muckle they may grieve ye.
For care and trouble set your thought,
    Even when your end's attained;
And a' your views may come to nought,
    Where every nerve is strained.

I'll no say men are villains a';
    The real, hardened wicked,
Wha hae nae check but human law,
    Are to a few restricked:
But, och! mankind are unco weak,
    And little to be trusted;
If self the wavering balance shake,
    It's rarely right adjusted!

Yet they wha fa' in fortune's strife,
 Their fate we shouldna censure,
For still th' important end of life
 They equally may answer:
A man may hae an honest heart,
 Though poortith hourly stare him;
A man may tak a neebor's part,
 Yet hae nae cash to spare him.

Aye free, aff han' your story tell,
 When wi' a bosom crony;
But still keep something to yoursel
 Ye scarcely tell to ony.
Conceal yoursel as weel's ye can
 Frae critical dissection,
But keek through every other man.
 Wi' sharpened, sly inspection.

The sacred lowe o' weel-placed love,
 Luxuriantly indulge it;
But never tempt th' illicit rove,
 Though naething should divulge it.
I waive the quantum o' the sin,
 The hazard o' concealing;
But, och! it hardens a' within,
 And petrifies the feeling!

To catch Dame Fortune's golden smile,
 Assiduous wait upon her;
And gather gear by every wile
 That's justified by honor;
Not for to hide it in a hedge,
 Nor for a train-attendant,
But for the glorious privilege
 Of being independent.

The fear o' hell's a hangman's whip,
    To haud the wretch in order;
But where ye feel your honor grip,
    Let that aye be your border:
Its slightest touches, instant pause—
    Debar a' side-pretences;
And resolutely keep its laws,
    Uncaring consequences.

The great Creator to revere
    Must sure become the creature;
But still the preaching cant forbear,
    And even the rigid feature.
Yet ne'er with wits profane to range,
    Be cómplaisance extended;
An Atheist laugh's a poor exchange
    For Deity offended!

When ranting round in Pleasure's ring,
    Religion may be blinded;
Or if she gie a random sting,
    It may be little minded;
But when on life we're tempest-driven,
    A conscience but a canker,
A correspondence fixed wi' Heaven
    Is sure a noble anchor!

Adieu, dear, amiable youth!
    Your heart can ne'er be wanting!
May prudence, fortitude, and truth,
    Erect your brow undaunting!
In ploughman phrase, "God send you speed,"
    Still daily to grow wiser;
And may you better reck the rede
    Than ever did th' adviser!

THE WANDERER

Eugene Field
1850-1895

Field is said to have written The Wanderer in kindly banter of the son of the great actress Helena Modjeska, an eminent engineer who could build great bridges but not overcome his homesickness for his native Poland. Its half playful origin does affect its poetic value.

Upon a mountain height, far from the sea,
    I found a shell,
And to my listening ear the lonely thing
Ever a song of ocean seemed to sing,
    Ever a tale of ocean seemed to tell.

How came the shell upon the mountain height?
    Ah, who can say
Whether there dropped by some too careless hand,
Or whether there cast when ocean swept the land,
    Ere the Eternal ordained the Day?

Strange, was it not? Far from its native deep,
    One song it sang,—
Sang of the awful mysteries of the tide,
Sang of the misty sea, profound and wide,—
    Ever with echoes of the ocean rang.

And as the shell upon the mountain height
    Sings of the sea,
So do I ever, leagues and leagues away,—
So do I ever, wandering where I may,—
    Sing O my home! sing O my home! of thee.

A HERO
Florence Earle Coates
1850-1927

Mrs. Coates' own definition: "The business of Art is to enlarge and correct the heart ...to appeal to the soul."

In her many appeals for the open face of courage, her work simulates the philosophy of the Japanese people who hide an aching heart behind a cheerful countenance. Like Roselle Mercier Montgomery (p. 109) she refuses "to make a garment of her grief."

> *"For death in patriot fight may be*
> *Less gallant than a smile."*

He sang of joy; whate'er he knew of sadness
    He kept for his own heart's peculiar share:
So well he sang, the world imagined gladness
    To be sole tenant there.

For dreams were his, and in the dawn's fair shining,
    His spirit soared beyond the mounting lark;
But from his lips no accent of repining
    Fell when the days grew dark;

And though contending long dread Fate to master,
    He failed at last her enmity to cheat,
He turned with such a smile to face disaster
    That he sublimed defeat.

THE WORLD'S NEEDS
Ella Wheeler Wilcox
1855-1919

So many gods, so many creeds,
    So many paths that wind and wind,
    While just the art of being kind
Is all this sad world needs.

THE SPIRES OF OXFORD
Winifred M. Letts

Winifred Letts, an Irish girl, author, and poet, knows first hand of the boys who left the cricket field to seek a bloody sod, for she was a nurse in the Great War.

Oxford, one of the famous old British universities, gave its youth, direct from the bloom of life to the tomb of martyrdom. One thinks of Newbolt's Lampada Vitae:

Every one of her sons must hear
And none that hears it dares forget.

I saw the spires of Oxford
    As I was passing by,
The gray spires of Oxford
    Against the pearl-gray sky;
My heart was with the Oxford men
    Who went abroad to die.

The years go fast in Oxford.
    The golden years and gay,
The hoary Colleges look down
    On careless boys at play.
But when the bugles sounded—*War!*
    They put their games away.

They left the peaceful river,
    The cricket field, the quad,
The shaven lawns of Oxford,
    To seek a bloody sod.
They gave their merry youth away
    For country and for God.

God rest you, happy gentlemen,
    Who laid your good lives down,
Who took the khaki and the gun
    Instead of cap and gown.
God bring you to a fairer place
    Than even Oxford town.

OPPORTUNITY

Walter Malone

1866-1915

There are four well-known poems of the title Opportunity: of Sill, wherein the king's son caught up the flung sword, "lifted it afresh and hewed his enemy down"; of Markham,—

> *In an old city by the storied shores*
> *Where the bright summit of Olympus soars . . ;"*

of Ingalls,—

> *...but those who doubt or hesitate,*
> *Condemned to failure, penury, and woe,*
> *Seek me in vain and uselessly implore—*
> *I answer not, and I return no more;*

and this now famous verse of the Memphis (Tenn.) jurist and author, Walter Malone. This poem was written before that of Ingalls and therefore is not a reply to it.

They do me wrong who say I come no more
    When once I knock and fail to find you in;
For every day I stand outside your door,
    And bid you wake, and rise to fight and win.

Wail not for precious chances passed away,
    Weep not for golden ages on the wane!
Each night I burn the records of the day,—
    At sunrise every soul is born again!

Laugh like a boy at splendors that have sped,
    To vanished joys be blind and deaf and dumb;
My judgments seal the dead past with its dead,
    But never bind a moment yet to come.

Though deep in mire, wring not your hands and weep;
    I lend my arm to all who say "I can!"
No shame-faced outcast ever sank so deep,
    But yet might rise and be again a man!

Dost thou behold thy lost youth all aghast?
　　Dost reel from righteous Retribution's blow?
Then turn from blotted archives of the past,
　　And find the future's pages white as snow.

Art thou a mourner? Rouse thee from thy spell;
　　Art thou a sinner? Sins may be forgiven;
Each morning gives thee wings to flee from hell,
　　Each night a star to guide thy feet to heaven.

TEARS*

Lizette Woodworth Reese

1856-

Lizette Woodworth Reese was for almost half a century a teacher in the public schools of Baltimore. After her retirement in May, 1923, friends dedicated a bronze tablet of her most famous poem, Tears, in the halls of the Western High School where she had taught for twenty years.

When I consider Life and its few years—
A wisp of fog betwixt us and the sun;
A call to battle, and the battle done
Ere the last echo dies within our ears;
A rose choked in the grass; an hour of fears;
The gusts that past a darkening shore do beat;
The burst of music down an unlistening street—
I wonder at the idleness of tears.
Ye old, old dead, and ye of yesternight,
Chieftains, and bards, and keepers of the sheep,
By every cup of sorrow that you had,
Loose me from tears, and make me see aright
How each hath back what once he stayed to weep;
Homer his sight, David his little lad!

UNEASY LIES THE HEAD

William Shakspere

1564-1616

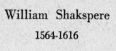

Shakspere has much to say of sleep—of sweet voices
> *That, if I then had wak'd after long sleep,*
> *Will make me sleep again. (Tempest)*
And in such a voice Romeo soothes the gentle Juliet—
> *Sleep dwell upon thine eyes, peace in thy breast!*
> *Would I were sleep and peace, so sweet to rest!*
Now terror-stricken Macbeth, murdered blood upon his palms, cries out—
> *Methought I heard a voice cry,*
> *"Sleep no more!"*
> *Macbeth does murder sleep,—the innocent sleep,*
> *Sleep that knits up the ravell'd sleave of care,*
> *The death of each day's life, sore labour's bath,*
> *Balm of hurt minds, great nature's second course,*
> *Chief nourisher in life's feast,—*
And from—
> *Downy sleep, death's counterfeit (Macbeth)*
Shakspere turns to death itself.
> *Duncan is in his grave;*
> *After life's fitful fever he sleeps well.*
> *Treason has done his worst; nor steel nor poison,*
> *Malice domestic, foreign levy, nothing*
> *Can touch him further. (Macbeth)*
But here is the famous fret of sleeplessness from 2 Henry IV—

> How many thousand of my poorest subjects
> Are at this hour asleep! O sleep! O gentle sleep!
> Nature's soft nurse, how have I frighted thee,
> That thou no more wilt weigh my eyelids down
> And steep my senses in forgetfulness?
> Why rather, sleep, liest thou in smoky cribs,
> Upon uneasy pallets stretching thee,
> And hushed with buzzing night-flies to thy slumber,

Than in the perfumed chambers of the great,
Under the canopies of costly state,
And lulled with sound of sweetest melody?
O thou dull god! why liest thou with the vile
In loathsome beds, and leav'st the kingly couch
A watch-case or a common 'larum bell?
Wilt thou upon the high and giddy mast
Seal up the ship-boy's eyes, and rock his brains
In cradle of the rude imperious surge,
And in the visitation of the winds,
Who take the ruffian billows by the top,
Curling their monstrous heads, and hanging them
With deaf'ning clamor in the slippery clouds,
That with the hurly death itself awakes?
Canst thou, O partial sleep! give thy repose
To the wet sea boy in an hour so rude,
And in the calmest and most stillest night,
With all appliances and means to boot,
Deny it to a king? Then, happy low, lie down!
Uneasy lies the head that wears a crown.

IF STILL THEY LIVE

Edith M. Thomas

1854-1925

I feel my immortality o'ersweep all pains, all tears, all time, all fears; and peal, like the eternal thunders of the deep, into my ears this truth—thou livest forever!—Byron.

If still they live, whom touch nor sight
    Nor any subtlest sense can prove,
Though dwelling past our day and night,
    At farthest star's remove.—

Oh, not because these skies they change
    For upper deeps of sky unknown,
Shall that which made them ours grow strange,
    For spirit holds its own;

Whether it pace this earth around,
    Or cross, with printless, buoyant feet,
The unreverberant Profound
    That hath no name nor mete.

THE LAST TOURNEY

Frederic F. Van de Water

1890-

Inspiration and courage are complementary. Here is the call to courage,—the fearlessness of Bayard, Le chevalier sans peur et sans reproche, honored in death by his enemies; the faith of Roland, commanding the ill-fated rear guard of Charlemagne's army crossing the Pyrenees, whose horn, though futile, rang defiance.

I shall go forth some day to joust with Death
    I shall go forth when these alone abide:
        Old, rusted hopes and visions, cracked and dried.
I shall go forth and hear his slughorn's breath
Awake harsh echoes on the barren heath;
        Then for one flaming moment I shall ride
    The lists' brief course to meet the Undefied
And take the blow that I must fall beneath.

Each day, I gird my feeble soul with prayer:
    May then the blood of Bayard be mine own.
May I ride hard and true and smite him square
    And in a clash of arms be overthrown
    And, falling, hear upon the evening air
The distant horn of Roland, faintly blown.

THE MYSTIC
Cale Young Rice
1874-

Rice, a Kentuckian by birth and residence, is a prolific writer of plays, novels and poems. Where Science meets Religion, there it is that Beyond lies God. The Mystic somewhat resembles Carruth's "And others call it God."

There is a quest that calls me,
    In nights when I am alone,
The need to ride where the ways divide
    The Known from the Unknown.
I mount what thought is near me
    And soon I reach the place,
The tenuous rim where the Seen grows dim
    And the Sightless hides its face.

I have ridden the wind,
I have ridden the sea,
I have ridden the moon and stars,
I have set my feet on a stirrup-seat
Of a comet coursing Mars.
And everywhere
Thro' the earth and air
My thought speeds, lightning-shod,
It comes to a place, where checking pace
It cries, "Beyond lies God!"

It calls me out of the darkness,
    It calls me out of sleep,
"Ride! ride! for you must, to the end of Dust!"
    It bids and on I sweep

To the wide outposts of Being,
    Where there is Gulf alone—
And thro' a Vast that was never passed
    I listen for Life's tone.

I have ridden the wind,
I have ridden the night,
I have ridden the ghosts that flee
From the vaults of death like a chilling breath
Over eternity.
And everywhere
Is the earth laid bare—
Ether and star and clod—
Until I wind to its brink and find
But the cry, "Beyond lies God!"

It calls me and ever calls me!
    And vainly I reply,
"Fools only ride where the ways divide
    What Is from the Whence and Why!"
I'm lifted into the saddle
    Of thoughts too strong to tame
And down the deeps and over the steeps
    I find—ever the same.

I have ridden the wind,
I have ridden the stars,
I have ridden the force that flies
With far intent thro' the firmament
And each to each allies.
And everywhere
That a thought may dare
To gallop, mine has trod—
Only to stand at last on the strand
Where just beyond lies God.

THE PARTING GUEST*
James Whitcomb Riley
1849-1916

Riley said Good night at his home on Lockerbie Street, Indianapolis, July 22, 1916. The Riley Hospital, the largest children's hospital in the world, is maintained there in perpetuation of his love.

What delightful hosts they are—
    Life and Love!
Lingeringly I turn away,
    This late hour, yet glad enough
They have not withheld from me
    Their high hospitality.
So, with face lit with delight
    And all gratitude, I stay
    Yet to press their hands and say,
"Thanks,—So fine a time! Good night."

 # TO JAMES WHITCOMB RILEY
Bide Dudley
1877-

On the day of Riley's funeral this poem ran in an Indianapolis paper.

Well, good-by, Jim; take keer yerself;
    You've crossed the Great Divide.
Yer with that dear old sweetheart, Jim
    There on the other side.
A tear's in Orphant Annie's eye,
    A lump's in Sifer's throat,
An', Jim, they's quite a raft of us
    That's in the same old boat.

Well, good-by, Jim; take keer yerself!
    Yer dead, but still you'll live
In human hearts as long as God
    Has human life to give.
You b'longed to Him, Jim, anyway,
    An' you was only lent:
A nation's everlastin' love
    Shall be yer monument.

THE TWO FRIENDS

Charles Godfrey Leland

1824-1903

Charles Godfrey Leland is best known by the pen name of Hans Breitman. His was the age of the dialect poem, but it is for his standard English writings that he will be remembered.

I have two friends—two glorious friends—
    better could not be,
And every night when midnight tolls they
    meet to laugh with me.

The first was shot by Carlist thieves—
    ten years ago in Spain.
The second drowned near Alicante—while
    I alive remain.

I love to see their dim white forms come
    floating through the night,
And grieve to see them fade away in early
    morning light.

The first with gnomes in the Under Land
    is leading a lordly life,
The second has married a mermaiden, a
    beautiful water-wife.

And since I have friends in the Earth and
    Sea—with a few, I trust, on high,
'Tis a matter of small account to me—the
    way that I may die.

For whether I sink in the foaming flood,
    or swing on the triple tree,
Or die in my bed, as a Christian should,
    is all the same to me.

THE ZEST OF LIFE

Henry van Dyke

1852-1933

At the time of his death Henry van Dyke was easily dean of American poets. His poems are known for the fine courage of his fine, long, useful life. He served mankind as clergyman, minister of the United States to Netherlands and other European countries, and as head of the department of literature in Princeton University.

Let me but live my life from year to year,
    With forward face and unreluctant soul;
    Not hastening to, nor turning from the goal;
Not mourning for the things that disappear
In the dim past, nor holding back in fear
    From what the future veils; but with a whole
    And happy heart, that pays its toll
To Youth and Age, and travels on with cheer.

So let the way wind up the hill or down,
    O'er rough or smooth, the journey will be joy:
    Still seeking what I sought when but a boy,
New friendship, high adventure, and a crown,
    My heart will keep the courage of the quest,
    And hope the road's last turn will be the best.

AULD DADDY DARKNESS

James Ferguson

18—

Little is known of the author. Though the history of James Ferguson has vanished backward, the popularity of his Auld Daddy Darkness appreciates with the years.

Frae, from, is pronounced "fray"; *lowes* is to flame; *a'* is said like the first part of its meaning, all; and *claes,* clothes, is "clays.". A *gaffer* is a taskmaster, and *ca'* is drive.

Auld Daddy Darkness creeps frae his hole,
Black as a blackamoor, blin' as a mole:
Stir the fire till it lowes, let the bairnie sit
Auld Daddy Darkness is no wantit yit.

See him in the corners hidin' frae the licht,
See him at the window gloomin' at the nicht;
Turn up the gas licht, close the shutters a',
An' Auld Daddy Darkness will flee far awa'.

Awa' to hide the birdie within its cozy nest,
Awa' to lap the wee flooers on their mither's breast,
Awa' to loosen Gaffer Toil frae his daily ca',
For Auld Daddy Darkness is kindly to a'.

He comes when we're weary to wean's frae oor waes,
He comes when the bairnies are getting aff their claes;
To cover them sae cosy, an' bring bonnie dreams,
So Auld Daddy Darkness is better than he seems.

Steek yer een, my wee tot, ye'll see Daddy then;
He's in below the bed claes, to cuddle ye he's fain;
Noo nestle to his bosie, sleep and dream yer fill,
Till Wee Davie Daylicht comes keekin' owre the hill.

THE BARS OF FATE

Ellen M. H. Gates
1834-1920

*Unlike so many inspirational verses, these by Ellen M. H. Gates are poetry.
The setting is as clearly drawn as if on canvas, and lines gracefully natural.*

I stood before the bars of Fate
And bowed my head disconsolate;
So high they seemed, so fierce their frown.
I thought no hand could break them down.

Beyond them I could hear the songs
Of valiant men who marched in throngs;
And joyful women, fair and free,
Looked back and waved their hands to me.

I did not cry "Too late! too late!"
Or strive to rise, or rail at Fate,
Or pray to God. My coward heart,
Contented, played its foolish part.

So still I sat, the tireless bee
Sped o'er my head, with scorn for me,
And birds who build their nests in air
Beheld me, as I were not there.

From twig to twig, before my face,
The spiders wove their curious lace,
As they a curtain fine would see
Between the hindering bars and me.

Then, sudden change! I heard the call
Of wind and wave and waterfall;
From heaven above and earth below
A clear command—"ARISE AND GO!"

I upward sprang in all my strength,
And stretched my eager hands at length
To break the bars—no bars were there;
My fingers fell through empty air!

I RESOLVE

Charlotte Perkins Gilman

1860-1934

Mrs. Gilman, a descendant of the family of Lyman Beecher, is known for her attitude of happy stoicism, "never to look behind me for an hour." Consider the eternal youth of one who keeps a resolve always to think from the present forward, never backward. Errors are closed; there is no "might have been"; with Henry van Dyke—

> *"My heart will keep the courage of the quest*
> *......will never lose life's zest,*
> *And hope the road's last turn will be the best."*

To keep my health;
To do my work;
To live;
To see to it I grow and gain and give;
Never to look behind me for an hour;
To wait in meekness, and to walk in power;
But always fronting onward to the light,
Always and always facing toward the right.
Robbed, starved, defeated, fallen, wide-astray—
On, with what strength I have; ·
Back to the way.

THE OLD CLOCK ON
THE STAIRS

Henry W. Longfellow
1807-1882

"And in the hush that followed the prayer,
Was heard the old clock on the stair."

Somewhat back from the village street
Stands the old-fashioned country-seat.
Across its antique portico
Tall poplar-trees their shadows throw;
And from its station in the hall
An ancient timepiece says to all,—
  "Forever—never!
  Never—forever!"

Half-way up the stairs it stands,
And points and beckons with its hands
From its case of massive oak,
Like a monk, who, under his cloak,
Crosses himself, and sighs, alas!
With sorrowful voice to all who pass,—
  "Forever—never!
  Never—forever!"

By day its voice is low and light;
But in the silent dead of night,
Distinct as a passing footstep's fall,
It echoes along the vacant hall,
Along the ceiling, along the floor,
And seems to say, at each chamber-door,—
  "Forever—never!
  Never—forever!"

Through days of sorrow and of mirth,
Through days of death and days of birth,

Through every swift vicissitude
Of changeful time, unchanged it has stood,
And as if, like God, it all things saw,
It calmly repeats those words of awe,—
   "Forever—never!
   Never—forever!"

In that mansion used to be
Free-hearted Hospitality;
His great fires up the chimney roared;
The stranger feasted at his board;
But, like the skeleton at the feast,
That warning timepiece never ceased,—
   "Forever—never!
   Never—forever!"

There groups of merry children played,
There youths and maidens dreaming strayed;
O precious hours! O golden prime,
And affluence of love and time!
Even as a miser counts his gold,
Those hours the ancient timepiece told,—
   "Forever—never!
   Never—forever!"

From that chamber, clothed in white,
The bride came forth on her wedding night;
There, in that silent room below,
The dead lay in his shroud of snow;
And in the hush that followed the prayer
Was heard the old clock on the stair,—
   "Forever—never!
   Never—forever!"

All are scattered now and fled,
Some are married, some are dead;
And when I ask, with throbs of pain,
"Ah! when shall they all meet again?"
As in the days long since gone by,
The ancient timepiece makes reply,—
   "Forever—never!
   Never—forever!"

Never here, forever there,
Where all parting, pain, and care,
And death, and time, shall disappear,—
Forever there, but never here!
The horologe of Eternity
Sayeth this incessantly,—
"Forever—never!
Never—forever!"

ONE FIGHT MORE

Theodosia Garrison

1874-

*Here is delicacy of poetic art wedded to dauntless will. The last two lines
are unsurpassed in English poetry.*

Now, think you, Life, I am defeated quite?
    More than a single battle shall be mine
Before I yield the sword and give the sign
    And turn, a crownless outcast, to the night.
Wounded, and yet unconquered in the fight,
    I wait in silence till the day may shine
Once more upon my strength, and all the line
    Of your defenses break before my might.

Mine be that warrior's blood who, stricken sore,
    Lies in his quiet chamber till he hears
Afar the clash and clang of arms, and knows
    The cause he lived for calls for him once more;
And straightway rises, whole and void of fears,
    And arméd, turns him singing to his foes.

DEATH I CAN UNDERSTAND
Anonymous

Poetry is ever a surprising source of lovely pictures and satisfying thoughts. How different from the morbid forebodings on the Great Adventure is this:

Death I can understand.
If you had died I still might know content,
Believing, in that world where Here and
    There are blent,
To find you all unchanged. To check
    Life's gauge
With Death is to remain forever at that age
On earth attained. But what Fate planned
This grief? And why, at Life's not Death's
    demand,
Must we, who know the lovely art
Of soul-in-soul completeness, part—
But both live on, grow old and change?
It is this Life, so sadly strange,
I cannot understand.

IMMORTAL CRAFTSMEN
Daniel Webster
1782-1852

Great oratory is often great poetry.

If we work upon marble, it will perish;
If we work upon brass, time will efface it;
If we rear temples, they will crumble into dust;
But if we work upon immortal souls,
If we imbue them with principles,
With the just fear of the Creator and love of fellow men,
We engrave on those tablets something which will brighten
    all eternity.

I AM THE DOOR

Anonymous

Then said Jesus unto them again, verily, verily,
I say unto you, I am the door of the sheep.
—St. John 10:7.

A traveler once, when skies were rose and gold
With Syrian sunset, paused beside the fold
Where an Arabian shepherd housed his flock;
Only a circling wall of rough, grey rock—
No door, no gate, but just an opening wide
Enough for snowy, huddling sheep to come inside.
"So," questioned he, "then no wild beasts you dread?"
"Ah, yes, the wolf is near," the shepherd said.
"But"—strange and sweet the words Divine of yore
Fell on his startled ear: "I am the door!
When skies are sown with stars, and I may trace
The velvet shadows in this narrow space,
I lay me down. No silly sheep may go
Without the fold but I, the shepherd, know.
Nor need my cherished flock close-sheltered, warm,
Fear ravening wolf, save o'er my prostrate form."
O word of Christ—illumined evermore
For us, his timid sheep—"I am the door!"

COWARDS

William Shakspere
1564-1616

Cowards die many times before their deaths:
The valiant never taste of death but once.
Of all the wonders that I yet have heard,
It seems to me most strange that men should fear;
Seeing that death, a necessary end,
Will come, when it will come.

EN GARDE, MESSIEURS

William Lindsay

1858-1922

Most poems make the grand virtue self-abnegation. It may be well to read one with a different point of view. On guard, gentlemen, is addressed to gentlemen and implies fair play and vigorous resistance, both consistent with forceful and useful living.

EN GARDE, Messieurs, too long have I endured,
    Too long with patience borne the world's rebuff;
    Now he who shoulders me shall find me rough;
The weakness of an easy soul is cured.

I've shouted, leathern-lunged, when fame or gold,
    Were won by others, turned to aid my friend;—
    Dull-pated ever,—but such follies end;
Only a fool's content, and in the cold.

My doublet is in tatters, and my purse
    Waves in the wind, light as my lady's fan;
    Only my sword is bright; with it I plan
To win success, or put my sword to nurse.

I wait no longer for the primal blow;
    Henceforth my stroke is first, I give offense;
    I claim no more an over-dainty sense,
I brook no blocking where I plan to go.

En garde, Messieurs! and if my hand is hard,
    Remember I've been buffeted at will;
    I am a whit impatient, and 'tis ill
To cross a hungry dog, Messieurs, en garde.

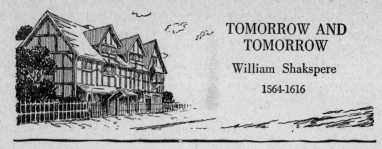

TOMORROW AND TOMORROW

William Shakspere
1564-1616

Three centuries of tomorrows have crept their petty pace of recorded time since Shakspere laid away the quill. Then why does he continue to hold first place in English literature? Passages like the following give the answer. The real mystery is, Where got this man so much of that Essence that time seems to accept as eternal? The passage is from Macbeth.

Tomorrow, and tomorrow, and tomorrow,
Creeps on this petty pace from day to day
To the last syllable of recorded time;
And all our yesterdays have lighted fools
The way to dusty death. Out, out, brief candle!
Life's but a walking shadow, a poor player
That struts and frets his hour upon the stage
And then is heard no more. It is a tale
Told by an idiot, full of sound and fury,
Signifying nothing.

PLAYS
Walter Savage Landor
1775-1864

And Landor follows Shakspere thus:

Alas, how soon the hours are over
Counted us out to play the lover.
And how much narrower is the stage
Allotted us to play the sage!
But when we play the fool, how wide
The theatre expands! beside,
How long the audience sits before us!
How many prompters! what a chorus!

CALLED BACK*
Emily Dickinson
1830-1886

Emily Dickinson, beloved of lovers of poetry, lived so much apart from worldly touch as to sing to us from some middle atmosphere. She lived and died in the house where she was born. She refused absolutely to allow publication of the little scraps of song written on little scraps of paper and handed, without comment to her sister; and it was not until 1890 that her work came to light. Her poems are like the rainbow, beautiful and ethereal, dissolving into the timelessness of starways.

Just lost when I was saved!
Just felt the world go by!
Just girt me for the onset with eternity,
When breath blew back
And on the other side
I heard recede the disappointed tide.

Therefore, as one returned, I feel,
Odd secrets of the line to tell!
Some sailor, skirting foreign shores,
Some pale reporter from the awful doors
Before the seal!

Next time, to stay!
Next time, the things to see
By ear unheard,
Unscrutinized by eye.

Next time, to tarry,
While the ages steal,—
Slow tramp the centuries,
And the cycles wheel.

* From "The Poems of Emily Dickinson," Centenary Edition. Edited by Martha Dickinson Bianchi and Alfred Leete Hampson. Reprinted by permission of Little, Brown & Company.

NEW EVERY MORNING*

Susan Coolidge
(Sarah Chauncey Woolsey)

1848-1894

Susan Coolidge was born in Cleveland, Ohio. She was the author of children's stories, chiefly The Katy Did Series.

Every day is a fresh beginning,
    Every morn is the world made new.
You who are weary of sorrow and sinning,
    Here is a beautiful hope for you,—
    A hope for me and a hope for you.

All the past things are past and over;
    The tasks are done and the tears are shed.
Yesterday's errors let yesterday cover;
    Yesterday's wounds, which smarted and bled,
    Are healed with the healing which night has shed.

Yesterday now is a part of forever,
    Bound up in a sheaf, which God holds tight,
With glad days, and sad days, and bad days, which never
    Shall visit us more with their bloom and their blight,
    Their fullness of sunshine or sorrowful night.

Let them go, since we cannot relive them,
    Cannot undo and cannot atone;
God in his mercy receive, forgive them!
    Only the new days are our own;
    To-day is ours, and to-day alone.

Here are the skies all burnished brightly,
    Here is the spent earth all reborn,
Here are the tired limbs springing lightly
    To face the sun and to share with the morn.
    In the chrism of dew and the cool of dawn.

*From *A Few More Verses*, by Susan Coolidge. Reprinted by permission of Little Brown & Company.

Every day is a fresh beginning,
    Listen, my soul, to the glad refrain,
And, spite of old sorrow and older sinning,
    The puzzles forecasted and possible pain,
    Take heart with the day, and begin again.

SONNET ON CHILLON

Lord Byron

1788-1824

Byron, with that passionate love for liberty that lured him to his death in 1824 in the Greek war of liberation, here pours out his art in commemoration of Francis Bonnivard, who for six years was imprisoned in the castle of Chillon near Montreux, Switzerland.

Eternal Spirit of the chainless Mind!
    Brightest in dungeons, Liberty! thou art,
    For there thy habitation is the heart—
The heart which love of thee alone can bind;

And when thy sons to fetters are consigned—
    To fetters, and the damp vault's dayless gloom,
    Their country conquers with their martyrdom,
And Freedom's fame finds wings on every wind.

Chillon! thy prison is a holy place,
    And thy sad floor an altar—for 't was trod,
Until his very steps have left a trace
    Worn, as if thy cold pavement were a sod,
By Bonnivard!—May none those marks efface!
    For they appeal from tyranny to God.

THE DEAD

Victor Starbuck
1887-1935

Victor Starbuck is an attorney in Asheville, North Carolina. He is the author of a volume, Wind Among the Pines.

The last four lines of The Dead are unforgetable, full of a massive figure that comprehends the soul.

I wonder do they sit in endless rest—
Plantagenet and Cromwell turned from wars,
Copernicus forgetful of the stars
And Milton mouthing but some outworn jest,
Drake and Columbus hugging harbor, lest
The tempest beat too loudly through their spars,
King David muttering over ancient scars,
His sling forgot, his chin upon his breast?

Believe it not. Still down the centuries
Go marching Saul, Navarre and Coeur de Lion;
And Shakespeare, polishing a new-made rhyme,
Lays by his quill to watch old argosies
Flash past the golden headlands of Orion,
Their sails a-flutter in the winds of time.

COMPANY

Richard R. Kirk
1877-

Thrice blessed are our friends: they come, they stay,
And presently they go away.

GRADATIM

J. G. Holland

1819-1881

Gradatim—step by step—has become a classic in inspirational literature. Holland was a practising physician and like so many others born to literature, he left his profession for the pen. He was the founder and first editor of The Century Magazine.

Heaven is not reached at a single bound;
    But we build the ladder by which we rise
    From the lowly earth to the vaulted skies,
And we mount to its summit, round by round.

I count this thing to be grandly true:
    That a noble deed is a step towards God,—
    Lifting the soul from the common clod
To a purer air and a broader view.

We rise by the things that are under feet;
    By what we have mastered of good and gain;
    By the pride deposed and the passion slain,
And the vanquished ills that we hourly meet.

We hope, we aspire, we resolve, we trust,
    When the morning calls us to life and light,
    But our hearts grow weary, and, ere the night,
Our lives are trailing the sordid dust.

We hope, we resolve, we aspire, we pray,
    And we think that we mount the air on wings
    Beyond the recall of sensual things,
While our feet still cling to the heavy clay.

Wings for the angels, but feet for men!
    We may borrow the wings to find the way—
    We may hope, and resolve, and aspire, and pray;
But our feet must rise, or we fall again.

Only in dreams is a ladder thrown
    From the weary earth to the sapphire walls;
    But the dreams depart, and the vision falls,
And the sleeper wakes on his pillow of stone.

Heaven is not reached at a single bound;
    But we build the ladder by which we rise
    From the lowly earth to the vaulted skies,
And we mount to its summit, round by round.

A LITTLE PRAYER

S. E. Kiser

Nothing in the prolific writings of the publicist and author, Samuel Ellsworth Kiser, surpasses his Little Prayer in—

    That best portion of a good man's life,
        His little, nameless, unremembered acts
        Of kindness and of love.
                    Wordsworth.

That I may not in blindness grope,
    But that I may with vision clear
Know when to speak a word of hope
    Or add a little wholesome cheer.

That tempered winds may softly blow
    Where little children, thinly clad,
Sit dreaming, when the flame is low,
    Of comforts they have never had.

That through the year which lies ahead
    No heart shall ache, no cheek be wet,
For any word that I have said
    Or profit I have tried to get.

TO A HURT CHILD

Grace Denio Litchfield

1849-

Grace Denio Litchfield was born in New York City but has spent much time abroad. She has written much excellent prose and poetry.

What, are you hurt, Sweet? So am I;
    Cut to the heart;
Though I may neither moan nor cry,
    To ease the smart.

Where was it, Love? Just here! So wide
    Upon your cheek!
Oh happy pain that needs no pride,
    And may dare speak.

Lay here your pretty head. One touch
    Will heal its worst,
While I, whose wound bleeds overmuch,
    Go all unnursed.

There, Sweet. Run back now to your play,
    Forget your woes.
I too was sorely hurt this day,—
    But no one knows.

 ## THRICE ARMED

William Shakspere

1564-1616

From 2 Henry VI, 3:2, 233.

Thrice is he armed that hath his quarrel just,
And he but naked, though locked up in steel,
Whose conscience with injustice is corrupted...

SO BE MY PASSING
William Ernest Henley
1849-1903

So Be My Passing and Invictus, "I am the captain of my soul," are the two best known of Henley's poems. This poem is sometimes called Margaritae Sorori and is one of the best loved in our literature.

A late lark twitters from the quiet skies
And from the west,
Where the sun, his day's work ended,
Lingers as in content,
There falls on the old, gray city
An influence luminous and serene,
A shining peace.

The smoke ascends
In a rosy-and-golden haze. The spires
Shine and are changed. In the valley
Shadows rise. The lark sings on. The sun,
Closing his benediction,
Sinks, and the darkening air
Thrills with a sense of the triumphing night—
Night with her train of stars
And her great gift of sleep.

So be my passing!
My task accomplish'd and the long day done,
My wages taken, and in my heart
Some late lark singing,
Let me be gather'd to the quiet west,
The sundown splendid and serene,
Death.

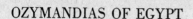

OZYMANDIAS OF EGYPT

Percy Bysshe Shelley
1792-1822

"When I consider Life and its few years—

* * * * * * * *

I wonder at the idleness of tears."

And at the idleness of over-reaching ambition, of intemperate acquisitiveness, of the gnatish things over which we harm one another, of man "who frets his hour upon the stage and then is heard no more"; for across it all tomorrow—
The lone and level sands stretch far away.

I met a traveller from an antique land
Who said: Two vast and trunkless legs of stone
Stand in the desert. Near them on the sand,
Half sunk, a shatter'd visage lies, whose frown
And wrinkled lip and sneer of cold command
Tell that its sculptor well those passions read
Which yet survive, stamp'd on these lifeless things,
The hand that mock'd them and the heart that fed;
And on the pedestal these words appear:
"My name is Ozymandias, king of kings:
Look on my works, ye Mighty, and despair!"

Nothing beside remains. Round the decay
Of that colossal wreck, boundless and bare,
The lone and level sands stretch far away.

WORDS

Alexander Pope
1688-1744

Words are like leaves; and where they most abound,
Much fruit of sense beneath is seldom found.

IF THIS WERE FAITH

Robert Louis Stevenson

1850-1894

NELSON WHITE

*Faith is not reason's labor, but re-
pose.—Young.*

God, if this were enough,
That I see things bare to the buff
And up to the buttocks in mire;
That I ask nor hope nor hire,
Nut in the husk,
Nor dawn beyond the dusk,
Nor life beyond death:
God, if this were faith?

Having felt thy wind in my face
Spit sorrow and disgrace,
Having seen thine evil doom
In Golgotha and Khartoum,
And the brutes, the work of thine hands,
Fill with injustice lands
And stain with blood the sea:
If still in my veins the glee
Of the black night and the sun
And the lost battle, run:
If, an adept,
The iniquitous lists I still accept
With joy, and joy to endure and be withstood,
And still to battle and perish for a dream of good:
God, if that were enough?
If to feel, in the ink of the slough,
And the sink of the mire,
Veins of glory and fire
Run through and transpierce and transpire,
And a secret purpose of glory in every part,

And the answering glory of battle fill my heart;
To thrill with the joy of girded men,
To go on forever and fail and go on again,
And be mauled to the earth and arise,
And contend for the shade of a word and a thing not
    seen with the eyes:
With the half of a broken hope for a pillow at night
That somehow the right is the right
And the smooth shall bloom from the rough:
Lord, if that were enough?

THE ROSE AND THE GARDENER

Austin Dobson

1840-1921

Beauty is like an almanack: if it last a year it is well.—T. Adams.

The Rose in the garden slipped her bud,
And she laughed in the pride of her youthful blood,
As she thought of the Gardener standing by—
"He is old—so old! And he soon must die!"

The full Rose waxed in the warm June air,
And she spread and spread till her heart lay bare;
And she laughed once more as she heard his tread—
"He is older now! He will soon be dead!"

But the breeze of the morning blew, and found
That the leaves of the blown Rose strewed the ground;
And he came at noon, that Gardener old,
And he raked them gently under the mould.

And I wove the thing to a random rhyme:
For the Rose is Beauty; the Gardener, Time.

I WILL LIFT UP MINE EYES
The Bible

Part of the One Hundred Twenty-first Psalm

I will lift up mine eyes unto the hills from
    whence cometh my help.
My help cometh from the Lord, which made
    Heaven and earth.
He will not suffer thy foot to be moved:
He that keepeth thee will not slumber.
Behold, He that keepeth Israel shall neither
    slumber nor sleep.
The Lord is thy keeper:
The Lord is thy shade upon thy right hand.
The sun shall not smite thee by day, nor the moon
    by night.
The Lord shall preserve thee from all evil:
He shall preserve thy soul.
The Lord shall preserve thy going out and thy
    coming in
From this time forth, and even for evermore.

 ## SIN IS SIN
Anonymous

*While the writer of this short poem is unknown, it is fairly evident that
the author is the mother of a boy.*

Don't send my boy where your girl can't go,
And say, "There's no danger for boys, you know,
Because they all have their wild oats to sow";
There is no more excuse for my boy to be low
Than your girl. Then please don't tell him so.

Don't send my boy where your girl can't go,
For a boy or a girl sin is sin, you know,
And my baby boy's hands are as clean and white,
And his heart as pure as your girl's tonight.

THE WISDOM OF FOLLY
Ellen Thornycroft Fowler
1860-1929

A merry heart goes all the day,
Your sad tires in a mile-a."
  —*Shakspere—Winters Tale.*

The cynics say that every rose
Is guarded by a thorn which grows
    To spoil our posies;
But I no pleasure therefore lack;
I keep my hands behind my back
    When smelling roses.

Though outwardly a gloomy shroud
The inner half of every cloud
    Is bright and shining;
I therefore turn my clouds about,
And always wear them inside out
    To show the lining.

My modus operandi this—
To take no heed of what's amiss;
    And not a bad one;
Because, as Shakespeare used to say,
A merry heart goes twice the way
    That tires a sad one.

AT THE CROSSROADS

Richard Hovey

1864-1900

Richard Hovey died at thirty-six. Yet in the few years given him, he, perhaps more than any other poet, helped to replace the stilted, poetic words and forms of mid-Victorian poetry with the free and expressive language of the new century.

You to the left and I to the right,
　　For the ways of men must sever—
And it well may be for a day and a night,
　　And it well may be forever.
But whether we meet or whether we part
　　(For our ways are past our knowing),
A pledge from the heart to its fellow heart
　　On the ways we all are going!
Here's luck!
　　For we know not where we are going.

We have striven fair in love and war,
　　But the wheel was always weighted!
We have lost the prize that we struggled for,
　　We have won the prize that was fated.
We have met our loss with a smile and a song,
　　And our gains with a wink and a whistle,—
For, whether we're right or whether we're wrong,
　　There's a rose for every thistle.
Here's luck!
　　And a drop to wet your whistle!

Whether we win or whether we lose
　　With the hands that life is dealing,
It is not we nor the ways we choose.
　　But the fall of the cards that's sealing.

There's a fate in love and a fate in fight,
   And the best of us all go under—
And whether we're wrong or whether we're right,
   We win, sometimes, to our wonder.
Here's luck!
   That we may not yet go under!

With a steady swing and an open brow
   We have tramped the ways together,
But we're clasping hands at the crossroads now
   In the Fiend's own night for weather;
And whether we bleed or whether we smile
   In the leagues that lie before us,
The ways of life are many a mile
   And the dark of Fate is o'er us.
Here's luck!
   And a cheer for the dark before us!

You to the left and I to the right,
   For the ways of men must sever,
And it well may be for a day and a night,
   And it well may be forever!
But whether we live or whether we die
   (For the end is past our knowing),
Here's two frank hearts and the open sky,
   Be a fair or an ill wind blowing!
Here's luck!
   In the teeth of all winds blowing.

STANDARDS

Charles Wharton Stork

1881-

White is the skimming gull on the somber
   green of the fir-trees,
Black is the soaring gull on a snowy
   glimmer of cloud.

THE SANDS OF DEE

Charles Kingsley

1819-1875

*At Chester the Dee flows northeastward into the western wind to the Irish
Sea. Dee, when the sea is out, is but a small river flowing thru a dreary waste
of land and ooze; but when the western tide flows round and round the sand the
cruel crawling foam reaches out to make Dee a dangerous arm of the ocean.*

"O Mary, go and call the cattle home,
    And call the cattle home,
    And call the cattle home
  Across the sands of Dee;"
The western wind was wild and dank with foam,
  And all alone went she.

The western tide crept up along the sand,
    And o'er and o'er the sand,
    And round and round the sand,
  As far as eye could see.
The rolling mist came down and hid the land:
  And never home came she.

"Oh! is it weed, or fish, or floating hair—
    A tress of golden hair,
    A drownèd maiden's hair
  Above the nets at sea?
Was never salmon yet that shown so fair
  Among the stakes on Dee."

They rowed her in across the rolling foam,
    The cruel crawling foam,
    The cruel hungry foam,
  To her grave beside the sea:
But still the boatmen hear her call the cattle home
  Across the sands of Dee.

SCYTHE SONG

Andrew Lang

1844-1912

Andrew Lang was an Englishman, a classicist of note, and the author of some poetry and numerous biological works. His best poetry is delicate light verse.

The younger generation will hardly have heard the swish of the scythe as the mower sweeps it in step. "Hush," drawn out, is perhaps the best word to describe its long sighing sound.

Mowers, weary and brown and blithe,
    What is the word methinks ye know,—
Endless over-word that the Scythe
    Sings to the blades of grass below?
Scythes that swing in the grass and clover,
    Something, still, they say as they pass;
What is the word that over and over,
    Sings the Scythe to the flowers and grass?

Hush, ah, hush, the Scythes are saying,
    Hush, and heed not, and fall asleep;
Hush they say to the grasses swaying;
    Hush they sing to the clover deep!
Hush—'tis the lullaby Time is singing—
    Hush, and heed not, for all things pass;
Hush, ah, hush! and the Scythes are swinging
    Over the clover, over the grass!

 # FROM HIS FIRST SONG

Robert Burns

1759-1796

She dresses aye so clean and neat,
    Baith decent and genteel,
And then there's something in her gait
    Gars ony dress look weel.

THE BELL BUOY

Rudyard Kipling
1865-

Born of Methodist missionaries in Bombay, educated in old England, resident with his American wife in Vermont, and now in England again; editor, writer of stories, poet, Kipling deserves the distinction Poet of the British Empire, whoever may be its poet laureate.

World traveler, he knew the sounds of ocean and of shore. It was probably on his return to England in 1897 that he gave language to the bell buoy as it rings warning of the shoal. "Dong! ding dong! ding dong!" said the bells of our childhood; but to Kipling, "Shoal! 'Ware shoal! 'Ware shoal!" He loves the bell buoy above the church bell, "my brother of old," tho "a saintly name he bears."

They christened my brother of old—
    And a saintly name he bears—
They gave him his place to hold
    At the head of the belfry stairs,
    Where the minster towers stand
And the breeding kestrels cry.
    Would I change with my brother a league inland?
Shoal! 'Ware shoal! Not I!

In the flush of the hot June prime,
    O'er smooth flood tides afire,
I hear him hurry the chime
    To the bidding of checked Desire;
    Till the sweated ringers tire
And the wild bob-majors die.
    Could I wait for my turn in the godly choir?
Shoal! 'Ware shoal! Not I!

When the smoking scud is blown,
    When the greasy wind rack lowers,
Apart and at peace and alone,
    He counts the changeless hours.

He wars with darkling Powers,
(I war with a darkling sea);
  Would he stoop to my work in the gusty mirk?
Shoal! 'Ware shoal! Not he!

There was never a priest to pray,
  There was never a hand to toll,
When they made me guard of the bay,
  And moored me over the shoal.
  I rock, I reel, and I roll—
My four great hammers ply—
  Could I speak or be still at the Church's will?
Shoal! 'Ware shoal! Not I!

The landward marks have failed,
  The fog bank glides unguessed,
The seaward lights are veiled,
  The spent deep feigns her rest:
  But my ear is laid to her breast,
I lift to the swell—I cry!
  Could I wait in sloth on the Church's oath?
Shoal! 'Ware shoal! Not I!

At the careless end of the night
  I thrill to the nearing screw;
I turn in the clearing light
  And I call to the drowsy crew;
  And the mud boils foul and blue
As the blind bow backs away.
  Will they give me their thanks if they clear the banks?
Shoal! 'Ware shoal! Not they!

The beach pools cake and skim,
  The bursting spray heads freeze,
I gather on crown and rim
  The gray, grained ice of the seas,
  Where, sheathed from bitt to trees,
The plunging colliers lie.
  Would I barter my place for the Church's grace?
Shoal! 'Ware shoal! Not I!

Through the blur of the whirling snow,
   Or the black of the inky sleet,
The lanterns gather and grow,
   And I look for the homeward fleet.
   Rattle of block and sheet—
"Ready about—stand by!"
   Shall I ask them a fee ere they fetch the quay?
Shoal! 'Ware shoal! Not I!

I dip and I surge and I swing
   In the rip of the racing tide,
By the gates of doom I sing,
   On the horns of death I ride.
   A ship length overside,
Between the course and the sand,
   Fretted and bound I bide
     Peril whereof I cry.
   Would I change with my brother a league inland?
Shoal! 'Ware shoal! Not I!

From "The Five Nations," by Rudyard Kipling. Used by special permission of Doubleday-Doran and Company and A. P. Watt & Son.

MY DAILY CREED
Anonymous

I will not be negligent to put you always in remembrance of these things, tho ye know them. Yea, I think it meet to stir you up by putting you in remembrance.— II Peter 1: 12-13.

Let me be a little kinder, let me be a little blinder
   To the faults of those about me; let me praise a little more;
Let me be, when I am weary, just a little bit more cheery;
   Let me serve a little better those that I am striving for...

Let me be a little braver when temptation bids me waver;
   Let me strive a little harder to be all that I should be;
Let me be a little meeker with the brother that is weaker;
   Let me think more of my neighbor and a little less of me.

I FEAR NO POWER A WOMAN WIELDS
Ernest McGaffey
1861-

*Ernest McGaffey, sometime lawyer of Chicago, was born in London, Ohio.
He is the author of Poems of Gun and Rod. This little poem will strike a
vibrant cord in the hearts of such as with Buel P. Colton love the "little
cabin folded in God's hills."*

I fear no power a woman wields
While I can have the woods and fields,
With comradeship alone of gun,
Gray marsh-wastes and the burning sun.

For aye the heart's most poignant pain
Will wear away 'neath hail and rain,
And rush of winds through branches bare
With something still to do and dare,—

The lonely watch beside the shore,
The wild-fowl's cry, the sweep of oar,
And paths of virgin sky to scan
Untrod, and so uncursed by man.

Gramercy, for thy haunting face,
Thy charm of voice and lissome grace,
I fear no power a woman wields
While I can have the woods and fields.

 ## SOLITUDE
William Allingham
1824-1889

Solitude is very sad,
Too much company twice as bad.

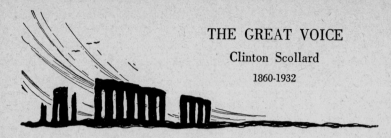

THE GREAT VOICE

Clinton Scollard

1860-1932

*Silence! The poet hears in the quiet of the desert earth's mightiest voice—
that speaks of God.*

I who have heard solemnities of sound—
The throbbing pulse of cities, the loud roar
Of ocean on sheer ledges of gaunt rock,
The chanting of innumerable winds
Around white peaks, the plunge of cataracts,
The whelm of avalanches, and, by night,
The thunder's panic breath—have come to know
What is earth's mightiest voice—the desert's voice—
Silence, that speaks with deafening tones of God.

IT MAY BE

S. E. Kiser

I had rather never receive a kindness than never bestow one.—Seneca.

It may be that you cannot stay
    To lend a friendly hand to him
Who stumbles on the slippery way,
    Pressed by conditions hard and grim;
It may be that you dare not heed
    His call for help, because you lack
The strength to lift him, but you need
    Not push him back.

It may be that he has not won
    The right to hope for your regard;
He may in folly have begun
    The course that he has found so hard;
It may be that your fingers bleed,
    That Fortune turns a bitter frown
Upon your efforts, but you need
    Not kick him down.

A FEAR

Ruth Messenger

Not more than once a year do we come across a sonnet worth keeping to read twice. We find such a sonnet, however, by Ruth Messenger, one of the cornhuskers who write for The Husk, published by the English classes of Cornell college, Mount Vernon, Iowa. Here it is:
—*Carl Sandberg, in the Chicago Daily News.*

It is not death I fear, nor that the gold
And pearl of early evening will outlast
This transient clay, and cooling shadows cast
Their quivering lengths into the self-same mold
And I not here; but that when I am old
And calm with the quiescence of desires
Long stilled, and stealthy quenching of youth's fires,
Evenings will come like this and leave me cold.

When cherry bloom shall only mean to me
Another canning season, and the deep
Untrodden snow a sidewalk to be swept;
Then will I face the darkness willingly,
And rather choose to sleep a dreamless sleep
Than cross, on bridges, streams that I have leapt.

AMERICA THE BEAUTIFUL

Katherine Lee Bates
1859-1929

Katherine Lee Bates, teacher, college professor, and author, has almost achieved the heights of a new American Anthem. America the Beautiful, though written in 1895 is doubtless now third in popular recognition following only America and The Star Spangled Banner.

The first lines of this great poem were written from a point half way up Pike's Peak when the author as she says, "looked out over the sea-like expanse of the fertile country spreading away so far under those ample skies." The complete poem first appeared in The Congregationalist, July 4, 1895, and won instant acclaim.

O beautiful for spacious skies,
    For amber waves of grain,
For purple mountain majesties
    Above the fruited plain!
      America! America!
    God shed his grace on thee
And crown thy good with brotherhood
    From sea to shining sea!

O beautiful for pilgrim feet,
    Whose stern, impassioned stress
A thoroughfare for freedom beat
    Across the wilderness!
      America! America!
    God mend thine every flaw,
Confirm thy soul in self-control,
    Thy liberty in law!

O beautiful for heroes proved
    In liberating strife,
Who more than self their country loved,
    And mercy more than life!

America! America!
May God thy gold refine
Till all success be nobleness
And every gain divine!

O beautiful for patriot dream
That sees beyond the years
Thine alabaster cities gleam
Undimmed by human tears!
America! America!
God shed His grace on thee
And crown thy good with brotherhood
From sea to shining sea!

THREE GATES

From the Arabian

Arabia and Japan, though far apart in space, race, tradition, and history, each recognize the humanity of the Golden Rule. Compare this fragment with the legend of the three little Japanese monkeys.

If you are tempted to reveal
A tale to you someone has told
About another, make it pass,
Before you speak, three gates of gold.
Three narrow gates: First, "Is it true?"
Then, "Is it needful?" In your mind
Give truthful answer. And the next
Is last and narrowest, "Is it kind?"
And if to reach your lips at last
It passes through these gateways three,
Then you may tell the tale, nor fear
What the result of speech may be.

HAPPINESS

Katherine Beeman

*This little poem is said to have
been written by a fifth grade child
in an American public school. The
point of view is hardly that of youth
—but the lines are poetry.*

This is a pleasant place between the hills;
I like the way the wide sky reaches down,
And gathers in the edges of the land
With one calm sweep of blue serenity;
I think that I will stop and tarry here
(For I have traveled long—not far, perhaps),
And watch those others, hastening as I used,
Along The Road, "The Road to Happiness!"

So let me stop, for I have not, before.
The others, surging onward toward—what goal?
Well, let them go. This place is very green;
And peace is here. And I am well content.

 ## PER ASPERA

Florence Earle Coates
1850-1927

*The motto of the state of Kansas is "Ad astra per aspera"—to the stars
over difficulties.*

Thank God, a man can grow!
    He is not bound
    With earthward gaze to creep along the ground:
Though his beginnings be but poor and low,
Thank God, a man can grow!
The fire upon his altars may burn dim,
    The torch he lighted may in darkness fail,
        And nothing to rekindle it avail,—
Yet high beyond his dull horizon's rim,
Arcturus and the Pleiads beckon him.

NEARER HOME

Phoebe Cary

1820-1871

Set to song, prayed with deepest fervor, known to millions, One Sweetly Solemn Thought is Phoebe Cary's monument.

One sweetly solemn thought
    Comes to me o'er and o'er;
I am nearer home today
    Than I ever have been before;

Nearer my Father's house,
    Where the many mansions be;
Nearer the great white throne,
    Nearer the crystal sea;

Nearer the bound of life,
    Where we lay our burdens down;
Nearer leaving the cross,
    Nearer gaining the crown.

But lying darkly between,
    Winding down through the night,
Is the silent, unknown stream,
    That leads at last to the light.

Closer and closer my steps
    Come to the dread abysm:
Closer Death to my lips
    Presses the awful chrism.

Oh, if my mortal feet
　　Have almost gained the brink;
If it be I am nearer home
　　Even today than I think;

Father, perfect my trust;
　　Let my spirit feel in death,
That her feet are firmly set
　　On the rock of living faith!

COURAGE

Amelia Earhart

1898-

It is as the first woman to fly the Atlantic alone that we best know Amelia Earhart. Behind the deed of daring we here discover the spring and philosophy of it in a poem that may well outlast contemporary fame.

Courage is the price that Life exacts for granting peace,
The soul that knows it not
Knows no release from little things:

Knows not the livid loneliness of fear,
Nor mountain heights where bitter joy can hear
The sound of wings.

How can Life grant us boon of living, compensate
For dull gray ugliness and pregnant hate
Unless we dare

The soul's dominion? Each time we make a choice,
　　we pay
With courage to behold resistless day,
And count it fair.

THE BELL
James Rorty
1890-

The very young may well afford to pass this poem by. Perhaps youth has not yet followed the beaten drum and the tambourine far enough to recognize their futility. But maturity needs the Bell ere confusion and disenchantment make its silver tones inaudible.

James Rorty—reporter, social worker, stretcher-bearer on the fields of France, editor, and playwright, was born at Middletown, New York, and is a graduate of Tufts. This poem may be slightly biographical.

On the day when I stopped begging at the heels of life,
On that day, as I sat on a high hill, looking at the sun,
I heard a bell strike far up in the sky, and my heart swelled,
And into my heart with laughter came trooping the lovely young-
  wise children of the wisdom of the earth.

Years had passed before that day; each year the circling seasons
  found me sad and mournful in the same place.
The fifes of spring played to me, the green grass cried to me, but
  I would not dance;
The winds of autumn tugged at me, but I would not sail;
Love found me frightened, questioning, and swept on.

In terror I fled to the schools, and pulling at the philosopher's
  beard, asked why, and why?
I listened respectfully to the wheeze and clatter of the editor's
  office;

I slept through the professor's lecture and humbly knew that I
  must be respectful, even while I slept.
There was not a drum beaten or a tambourine clashed anywhere,
  but I was there, beating time, beating time.

Until one day I heard a sweet bell pealing, far in the blue sky
    pealing, pealing,
And into my heart with laughter came trooping the lovely young-
    wise children of the wisdom of the earth.

It is long since I have seen the philosopher, but my laughing heart
    tells me he is still drawing triangles in the sky;
Having business elsewhere, I left the editor pleasuring in the midst
    of his favorite indignations;
Sitting at the foot of a stone, listening to the bluejays squalling wis-
    dom in the trees, I could find a pension in my heart for every
    professor in the world.

On the day when I stopped begging at the heels of life, lo,
The brown-robed mother of the western hills taught me quietness;
The blue-eyed mother of waters taught me peace.
Love shall have his toll of me; I have honey for every bee and
    seeds for every winging bird.

From "Children of the Sun and Other Poems," by James Rorty. Used by
permission of the Publishers, The Macmillan Company.

 ## THE GREATNESS OF THE SOUL

Alfred Tennyson

1809-1892

Everything here but the soul of man is a passing shadow.—Channing.

For tho' the Giant Ages heave the hill
And break the shore, and evermore
Make and break, and work their will;
Tho' world on world in myriad myriads roll
Round us, each with different powers,
And other forms of life than ours,
What know we greater than the soul?
On God and Godlike men we build our trust.

LIFE

Edward Rowland Sill

1841-1887

A short poem that epitomizes the life of its gentle teacher author.
Sill was class poet at Yale in 1861. Later he entered the Harvard Divinity School but gave up theology for teaching. At one time he was principal of the Oakland, California, high school and somewhat later, Professor of English at the University of California.

Forenoon and afternoon and night,—Forenoon,
And afternoon, and night,—Forenoon, and—what!
The empty song repeats itself. No more?
Yea, that is Life: make this forenoon sublime,
This afternoon a psalm, this night a prayer,
And Time is conquered, and thy crown is won.

DUSK

Clinton Scollard

1860-1932

Poet, critic, author, sometime Professor of Literature at Hamilton College.

Her feet along the dewy hills
    Are lighter than blown thistledown;
She bears the glamour of one star
    Upon her violet crown.

With her soft touch of mothering,
    How soothing to the sense she seems!
She holds within her gentle hand
    The quiet gift of dreams.

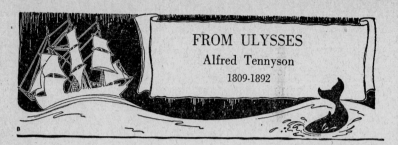

FROM ULYSSES
Alfred Tennyson
1809-1892

Arthur Hallam, friend of Tennyson, "passing the love of women," died suddenly in Vienna (1833). The tragedy threw Tennyson into a consideration of the deeper things of existence. His Break, Break, Break, is of Hallam. The picture of the aged Ulysses, determined to employ his remaining years in useful adventure, Tennyson tells us, was an expression of his own feeling of the necessity of pushing on after Hallam's death.

Ulysses is old. But not even his ten warring years before armed Troy, his perilous voyage home, the memories of a full life of dangers done have yet chilled the call of adventure within him. Leaving his wife, Penelope, and Telemachus, his reigning son, he rallies the veterans of his earlier years and bids them sail again.

Old age hath yet his honor and his toil.
Death closes all; but something ere the end,
Some work of noble note, may yet be done,
Not unbecoming men that strove with Gods.
The lights begin to twinkle from the rocks;
The long day wanes; the slow moon climbs; the deep
Moans round with many voices. Come, my friends.
'Tis not too late to seek a newer world.
Push off, and sitting well in order smite
The sounding furrows; for my purpose holds
To sail beyond the sunset, and the baths
Of all the western stars, until I die.
It may be that the gulfs will wash us down;
It may be we shall touch the Happy Isles,
And see the great Achilles, whom we knew.
Tho' much is taken, much abides; and tho'
We are not now that strength which in old days
Moved earth and heaven, that which we are, we are,—
One equal temper of heroic hearts,
Made weak by time and fate, but strong in will
To strive, to seek, to find, and not to yield.

THE TRUMPETER

Thomas Wentworth Higginson

1823-1911

Thomas Wentworth Higginson, critic, poet, author, was also a soldier. He was the first to command a colored regiment in the Civil War. He came from literary Cambridge (Mass.) and to Cambridge he returned to build for himself a second and more lasting fame.

I blew, I blew, the trumpet loudly sounding;
I blew, I blew, the heart within me bounding;
The world was fresh and fair, yet dark with wrong,
And men stood forth to conquer at the song—
       I blew! I blew! I blew!

The field is won, the minstrels loud are crying,
And all the world is peace, and I am dying.
Yet this forgotten life was not in vain;
Enough if I alone recall the strain,
       I blew! I blew! I blew!

THE GHOSTLY GALLEY
Jessie B. Rittenhouse

Miss Rittenhouse (Mrs. Clinton Scollard) has won fame in the fields of teaching, newspaper work, poetry, and authorship.

When comes the ghostly galley
    Whose rowers dip the oar
Without a sound to startle us,
    Unheeding on the shore,—

If they should beckon you aboard
    Before they beckon me,
How could I bear the waiting time
    Till I should put to sea!

A SONG OF LIFE

Angela Morgan

Angela Morgan was chosen to read her poem The Unknown Soldier over the bier of the nameless America hero as the body lay in state in the rotunda of the National Capitol. She also read her poem The Battle Cry of the Mothers at the Congress of Women at The Hague in 1915. She represents courage, freedom, womanhood.

Say not, "I live!"
    Unless the morning's trumpet brings
A shock of glory to your soul,
    Unless the ecstasy that sings
Through rushing worlds and insects' wings,
    Sends you upspringing to your goal,
Glad of the need for toil and strife,
    Eager to grapple hands with Life—
Say not, "I live!"

Say not, "I live!"
    Unless the energy that rings
Throughout this universe of fire
    A challenge to your spirit flings,
Here in the world of men and things,
    Thrilling you with a huge desire
To mate your purpose with the stars,
    To shout with Jupiter and Mars—
Say not, "I live!"

Say not, "I live!"
    Such were a libel on the Plan
Blazing within the mind of God
    Ere world or star or sun began.

Say rather, with your fellow man,
   "I grub; I burrow in the sod."
Life is not life that does not flame
    With consciousness of whence it came—
Say not, "I live!"

"I SHALL NOT MAKE A GARMENT OF MY GRIEF"

Roselle Mercier Montgomery

Roselle Mercier Montgomery (Mrs. John S.) wrote some excellent poetry in her youth in Georgia, but ceased writing at the time of her marriage. It is since her resumption of writing in 1920 that her best work has been done. Some of her work is under pen name of "Glen Allen."
   Benedick in Much Ado generalizes after the manner of men: "Everyone can master a grief but he who has it," but Mrs. Montgomery's poem is the voice of courage.

I shall not make a garment of my grief,
   Enshrouding me, for all the world to see;
But I shall wear grief as a secret charm,
   Where none may see—close to the heart of me!

I shall not go in mourning livery
   So that, as I pass by, the world will say:
"Behold a mourner!" Only night shall know
   My tears—I shall go smiling in the day!

Yet they who grieve shall know the charm is there,
   Close to my heart—my secret talisman!
And they will dry their eyes and smile at me,
   And understand—as but the grieving can!

THE HOMELAND

Dana Burnet

1888-

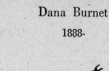

Home, the spot on earth supremely blest,
A dearer, sweeter spot than all the rest.
                                    —Montgomery.

My land was the west land; my home was on the hill.
I never think of my land but it makes my heart to thrill;
I never smell the west wind that blows the golden skies,
But old desire is in my feet and dreams are in my eyes.

My home crowned the high land; it had a stately grace.
I never think of my land but I see my mother's face;
I never smell the west wind that blows the silver ships,
But old delight is in my heart and mirth is on my lips.

My land was a high land; my home was near the skies.
I never think of my land but a light is in my eyes;
I never smell the west land that blows the summer rain,—
But I am at my mother's knee, a little lad again.

 ## PLAYING THE GAME

Anonymous

It isn't the fact that you're dead that counts,
But only how did you
                                    —Cooke.

Do you wilt and whine, if you fail to win
    In the manner you think your due?
Do you sneer at the man in case that he can
    And does, do better than you?
Do you take your rebuffs with a knowing grin?
    Do you laugh tho' you pull up lame?
Does your faith hold true when the whole world's blue?
    How are you playing the game?

INTERLUDE

Ella Wheeler Wilcox

1855-1919

Childhood itself is scarcely more lovely than a cheerful, kindly, sunshiny old age.—Child.

When in 1919 Ella Wheeler Wilcox went on alone there passed another of the kindly poets. It may be that she belonged more to the school of the nineteenth century, but it is equally true that the world has need of kindliness such as hers. Her verses have helped thousands to walk with a braver step.

The days grow shorter, the nights grow longer,
    The headstones thicken along the way;
And life grows sadder, but love grows stronger
    For those who walk with us, day by day.

The tear comes quicker, the laugh comes slower,
    The courage is lesser to do and dare;
And the tide of joy in the heart runs lower
    And seldom covers the reefs of care.

But all true things in the world seem truer,
    And the better things of the earth seem best;
And friends are dearer as friends are fewer,
    And love is all as our sun dips west.

Then let us clasp hands as we walk together,
    And let us speak softly, in love's sweet tone,
For no one knows, on the morrow, whether
    We two pass by, or but one alone.

A RHYME FOR THANKSGIVING DAY

Edwin Markham

1852-

Markham is the author of The Man with the Hoe, and Lincoln, the Man of the People. He is the poet of homey things, of kindness, and of courage.

I count up in this hour of cheer
The blessings of a busy year:

A roof so low I lose no strain,
No ripple of the friendly rain,
A chimney where all Winter long
The logs give back the wild bird's song.

The tree-toad that is first to cheer
With crinkling flute the green o' the year;
The cricket on the garden mound,
Stitching the dark with threads of sound.

The wind that cools my hidden spring
And sets my corn-field whispering,
And shakes with Autumn breath for me
Late apples from the apple-tree.

The shy paths darting thru the wheat,
Marked by the prints of little feet—
Gray squirrels on their thrifty round,
Crows condescending to the ground.

That leafy hollow that was stirred
A hundred mornings by a bird
Which sang at daybreak on a brier,
Setting the gray of dawn afire!

The lone star and the shadowed hush
That comes at evening, when the thrush
Turns with his wild heart all the long
Soft twilight to a mystic song.

The tender sorrow, too, that came
To leave me nevermore the same;
The love and memories and the wild
Light laughter of a little child.

And deep thanksgiving for the friend
Who came when all things seemed to end;
Whose courage helped me lift the load,
Whose spirit lit the darkened road.

WINDY NIGHTS

Robert Louis Stevenson

1850-1894

Windy Nights is one of the most apt fabrications in the language. It sur-
passes DeQuincey's fulminations in physical explanation of mental things.

Whenever the moon and stars are set,
  Whenever the wind is high,
All night long in the dark and wet,
  A man goes riding by.
Late in the night when the fires are out,
Why does he gallop and gallop about?

Whenever the trees are crying aloud.
  And ships are tossed at sea,
By, on the highway, low and loud,
  By at the gallop goes he.
By at the gallop he goes, and then
By he comes back at the gallop again.

A BALLAD OF HEROES

Austin Dobson

1840-1921

The heroes of mankind are the mountains, the highlands of the moral world.—Stanley.

Because you passed, and now are not,—
    Because, in some remoter day,
Your sacred dust from doubtful spot
    Was blown of ancient airs away,—
    Because you perished,—must men say
Your deeds were naught, and so profane
    Your lives with that cold burden? Nay,
The deeds you wrought are not in vain!

Though it may be, above the plot
    That hid your once imperial clay,
No greener than o'er men forgot
    The unregarding grasses sway;—
    Though there no sweeter is the lay
Of careless bird,—though you remain
    Without distinction of decay,—
The deeds you wrought are not in vain!

No. For while yet in tower or cot
    Your story stirs the pulses' play;
And men forget the sordid lot—
    The sordid care, of cities gray;—
    While yet, be-set in homelier fray,
They learn from you the lesson plain
    That Life may go, so Honor stay,—
The deeds you wrought are not in vain!

ENVOY

> Heroes of old! I humbly lay
>   The laurel on your graves again;
> Whatever men have done, men may,—
>   The deeds you wrought are not in vain.

MORS BENEFICA

Edmund Clarence Stedman

1833-1908

The same brave idea is expressed elsewhere in this volume in Let Me Live Out My Years, by John G. Neihardt.

The old man eloquent was doubtless Elijah snatched up into heaven while the sons of the Prophets looked on from a distance (II Kings, 2): and as the dying chief for whom victory a moment stayed, one thinks of Wolfe on the Heights of Abraham—"They run! Thank God; I die happy."

> Give me to die unwitting of the day,
>   And stricken in Life's brave heat, with senses clear:
>   Not swathed and couched until the lines appear
> Of Death's wan mask upon this withering clay,
> But as that old man eloquent made way
>   From Earth, a nation's conclave hushed anear;
>   Or as the chief whose fates, that he may hear
> The victory, one glorious moment stay.

> Or, if not thus, then with no cry in vain,
>   No ministrant beside to ward and weep,
> Hand upon helm I would my quittance gain
>   In some wild turmoil of the waters deep,
>   And sink content into a dreamless sleep
> (Spared grave and shroud) below the ancient main.

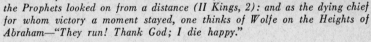

THE LION PATH

Charlotte Perkins Gilman
1860-

Our doubts are traitors,
And make us lose the good we oft might win
By fearing to attempt.
        —Shakspere—Measure for Measure.

I dare not!—
            Look! the road is very dark—
The trees stir softly and the bushes shake,
The long grass rustles, and the darkness moves
Here! there! beyond—!
There's something crept across the road just now!
And you would have me go—?
Go *there*, through that live darkness, hideous
With stir of crouching forms that wait to kill?
Ah, *look!* See there! and there! and there again!
Great yellow, glassy eyes, close to the ground!
Look! Now the clouds are lighter I can see
The long slow lashing of the sinewy tails,
And the set quiver of strong jaws that wait—!
Go there? Not I! Who dares to go who sees
So perfectly the lions in the path?

Comes one who dares.
            Afraid at first, yet bound
On such high errand as no fear could stay.
Forth goes he, with lions in his path.
And then—?
            He dared a death of agony—
Outnumbered battle with the king of beasts—
Long struggles in the horror of the night—

Dared, and went forth to meet—O ye who fear!
Finding an empty road, and nothing there—
A wide, bare, common road, with homely fields,
And fences, and the dusty roadside trees—
Some spitting kittens, maybe, in the grass.

IN THE PUBLIC LIBRARY

Alethea Todd Alderson

Men live in fancy who have died afoot.

I see them totter in, the very old,
    In clumsy, shapeless clothes and shabby shoes;
    With eager eyes they search the racks for news
Or seek the magazines where tales are told:
Strange tales of mystery and fairy gold,
    Romance, adventure, and the distant glow
    Of that far land where dreams forgotten go,
Where no one is neglected, hungry, cold.

Not all are old and poor; the young are here.
    With eager hearts they come to learn; 'tis plain
    They have the faith of youth, and its disdain
Of failure, disappointment, loss and fear.
    Some day, they too will watch the setting sun,
    And reading here, forget what life has done!

THE ETERNAL GOODNESS
John Greenleaf Whittier
1807-1882

The first poems of the Quaker farm boy found their way into the New-buryport Free Press edited by William Lloyd Garrison, the abolitionist. Impressed, the great liberator took the lad into his home and sent him to Haverhill Academy. The influence of Garrison and of Whittier's acknowledged literary mentor, Robert Burns, is doubtless responsible for the great quality of the brotherly love that pervades his poems, even to a gentle chiding of the teachers of an uncompromising religion that was so much a part of the thought of his day.

O friends! with whom my feet have trod
    The quiet aisles of prayer,
Glad witness to your zeal for God
    And love of man I bear.

I trace your lines of argument;
    Your logic linked and strong
I weigh as one who dreads dissent,
    And fears a doubt as wrong.

But still my human hands are weak
    To hold your iron creeds;
Against the words ye bid me speak
    My heart within me pleads.

Who fathoms the Eternal Thought?
    Who talks of scheme and plan?
The Lord is God! He needeth not
    The poor device of man.

I walk with bare, hushed feet the ground
   Ye tread with boldness shod;
I dare not fix with mete and bound
   The love and power of God.

Ye praise His justice, even such
   His pitying love I deem:
Ye seek a king; I fain would touch
   The robe that hath no seam.

Ye see the curse which overbroods
   A world of pain and loss;
I hear our Lord's beatitudes
   And prayer upon the cross.

*   *   *   *   *

No offering of my own I have,
   Nor works my faith to prove;
I can but give the gifts He gave,
   And plead His love for love.

And so beside the Silent Sea
   I wait the muffled oar;
No harm from Him can come to me
   On ocean or on shore.

I know not where His islands lift
   Their fronded palms in air;
I only know I cannot drift
   Beyond His love and care.

O brothers! if my faith is vain,
   If hopes like these betray,
Pray for me that my feet may gain
   The sure and safer way.

And Thou, O Lord! by whom are seen
   Thy creatures as they be,
Forgive me if too close I lean
   My human heart on Thee!

MY PRAYER
Elsie Janis

Every American boy "over there" will remember the incomparable service to America of the little actress Elsie Janis. Others will remember her as "The Slim Princess" and in vaudeville. And now here is a poem.

God let me live each lovely day,
    So I may know, that come what may:
I've done my best, to live the way,
    You want me to.

Forgive me if I do not pray.
    In church on every Sabbath day;
The ultra sanctimonious way,
    As some folks do.

Just let me know if I should stray,
    That I may stop along the way;
At any time of night or day,
    And talk to You.

 # GOOD DEEDS
William Shakspere
1564-1616

From Merchant of Venice, V:1, 90.

How far that little candle throws his beams!
So shines a good deed in a naughty world.
Heaven doth with us as we with torches do;
Not light them for themselves; for if our virtues
Did not go forth of us, 'twere all alike
As if we had them not.

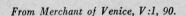

THEY SLEEP SO QUIETLY

Virginia Lyne Tunstall

Old Bruton, the oldest Episcopal Church in America, nestles in its shaded graveyard at Williamsburg, Virginia, once the capital of Colonial America, and often called the cradle of the Revolution. Old Bruton's bell rang for the repeal of the Stamp Act in 1766, and after the first act of sovereignty in America, six weeks before the Declaration of Independence, and again when Cornwallis surrendered at Yorktown, a few miles away.

In its graveyard lie the dead of early America, of Jamestown less than ten miles away, many of them born in England and come in youth to a new land and new hopes.

Mrs. Tunstall lives in Richmond.

They sleep so quietly, those English dead,
    In Bruton churchyard, when the cold wind sighs
Through the stripped branches, weaving overhead
    Fantastic webs against the wintry skies.
They do not heed the hurrying snow which covers
    Their unremembered names,—Margaret, and Joan,
Philip and Lucy, long forgotten lovers,—
    Where the white silence of the drifts is blown.

But when the hawthorn spills her petals down,
    And ranks of jonquils break in shining blooms
As April lingers in the little town,
    They will lie dreaming in the ancient tombs
Of Cornwall's cliffs beneath the soft spring rains,
Or foxgloves nodding in the Devon lanes.

THE TRAILING ARBUTUS

John Greenleaf Whittier
1807-1892

The trailing arbutus is a lovely, early spring flower found in woodsy places almost everywhere in eastern North America. Its flowers are pink, or sometimes delicately rose, and sometimes white, "tinted like a shell." It is called ground laurel in the south and sometimes the May flower in New England. In the sketch of his picturing, Whittier here approaches the art of modern poets.

I wandered lonely where the pine trees made
Against the bitter East their barricade,
    And, guided by its sweet
Perfume, I found, within a narrow dell,
The trailing spring bower tinted like a shell
    Amid dry leaves and mosses at my feet.

From under dead boughs, for whose loss the pines
Moaned ceaselessly overhead, the blossoming vines
    Lifted their glad surprise,
While yet the bluebird smoothed in leafless trees
His feathers ruffled by the chill sea breeze,
    And snow drifts lingered under April skies.

As, pausing, o'er the lonely flower I bent,
I thought of lives thus lowly, clogged and pent,
    Which yet find room,
Through care and cumber, coldness and decay,
To lend a sweetness to the ungenial day,
    And make the sad earth happier for their bloom.

MY WAGE

Jessie B. Rittenhouse

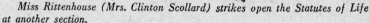

In his Bible, Sir Walter Raleigh wrote the night before his execution, October 29, 1618:

> *Even such is time that takes in trust*
> *Our youth, our joys, our all we have,*
> *And pays us with age and dust....*

Miss Rittenhouse (Mrs. Clinton Scollard) strikes open the Statutes of Life at another section.

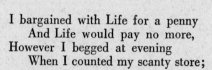

I bargained with Life for a penny
    And Life would pay no more,
However I begged at evening
    When I counted my scanty store;

For Life is a just employer,
    He gives you what you ask,
But once you have set the wages,
    Why, you must bear the task.

I worked for a menial's hire,
    Only to learn, dismayed,
That any wage I had asked of Life,
    Life would have paid.

THE STRUGGLE

Miriam Teichner

1888-

If I am asked who is the greatest man, I answer the best.—Sir William Jones.

Did you ever want to take your two bare hands,
    And choke out of the world your big success?
Beat, torn fists bleeding, pathways rugged, grand,
    By sheer brute strength and bigness, nothing less?

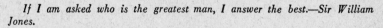

So at the last, triumphant, battered, strong,
    You might gaze down on what you choked and beat,
And say, "Ah, world, you've wrought to do me wrong;
    And thus have I accepted my defeat."

Have you ever dreamed of virile deeds, and vast,
    And then come back from deams with wobbly knees,
To find your way (the braver vision past),
    By picking meekly at typewriter keys;
By bending o'er a ledger, day by day,
    By some machine-like drudging? No great woe
To grapple with. Slow, painful is the way,
    And still, the bravest fight and conquer so.

NATURE

Henry W. Longfellow
1807-1882

*This is the hopeful philosophy of a gentle man
—to keep the joys of life half present in the peo-
pled world of memory while we look forward to
those that are yet newer and better.*

As a fond mother, when the day is o'er,
    Leads by the hand her little child to bed,
    Half willing, half reluctant to be led,
And leave his broken playthings on the floor,
Still gazing at them through the open door,
    Nor wholly reassured and comforted
    By promises of others in their stead,
Which, though more splendid, may not please him more;

So Nature deals with us, and takes away
    Our playthings one by one, and by the hand
    Leads us to rest so gently, that we go
Scarce knowing if we wished to go or stay,
    Being too full of sleep to understand
    How far the unknown transcends the what we know.

LOVE SLUMBERS ON

Percy Bysshe Shelley

1792-1822

*"Shelley was not only a great poet, but the forerunner of a new century,"
says Bates. He is to poetry what Schubert was to music, the originator of a
delicate and airy art.*

> Music, when soft voices die,
> Vibrates in the memory—
> Odours, when sweet violets sicken,
> Live within the sense they quicken.
>
> Rose leaves, when the rose is dead,
> Are heap'd for the beloved's bed;
> And so thy thoughts, when Thou art gone,
> Love itself shall slumber on.

SOMETIMES

Thomas S. Jones, Jr.

1882-

*Thomas S. Jones was sometime associate editor of The Pathfinder. He is
the author of The Voice of Silence.*

> Across the fields of yesterday
>   He sometimes comes to me,
> A little lad just back from play—
>   The lad I used to be.
>
> And yet he smiles so wistfully
>   Once he has crept within,
> I wonder if he hopes to see
>   The man I might have been.

HE WHOM A DREAM
HATH POSSESSED

Sheamus O'Sheel
1886-

Similar to Scollard's If Only the Dreams Abide is this poem by Sheamus O'Sheel, who, strange to say, was born and bred in New York City.
Dreams are the only enduring fabric. Democracy and Christianity are but dreams. Robert Emmet and Nathan Hale died for a Dream.

He whom a dream hath possessed knoweth no more of doubting,
For mist and the blowing of winds and the mouthing of words he
    scorns;
Not the sinuous speech of schools he hears, but a knightly shouting,
And never comes darkness down, yet he greeteth a million morns.

He whom a dream hath possessed knoweth no more of roaming;
All roads and the flowing of waves and the speediest flight he knows,
But wherever his feet are set, his soul is forever homing,
And going, he comes, and coming he heareth a call and goes.

He whom a dream hath possessed knoweth no more of sorrow,
At death and the dropping of leaves and the fading of suns he
    smiles,
For a dream remembers no past and scorns the desire of a morrow,
And a dream in a sea of doom sets surely the ultimate isles.

He whom a dream hath possessed treads the impalpable marches,
From the dust of the day's long road he leaps to a laughing star,
And the ruins of worlds that fall he views from eternal arches,
And rides God's battlefield in a flashing and golden car.

YOU HAVE TO BELIEVE

Douglas Malloch
1872-

Because of his poems of the lumber industry Malloch has come to be known as "The Poet of the Woods." He is also the poet of inspiration and the common life.
We have to believe, if we are to avoid cynicism.

> *I, too, have loved and lost; I, too, must often fight hard to keep a steadfast faith—but I must not let it go, for without faith there would be no light in all the world.—Helen Keller.*

You have to believe in happiness,
    Or happiness never comes.
I know that a bird chirps none the less
    When all that he finds is crumbs.
You have to believe the buds will blow
Believe in the grass in the days of snow;
    Ah, that's the reason a bird can sing—
    On his darkest day he believes in Spring.

You have to believe in happiness—
    It isn't an outward thing.
The Spring never makes the song, I guess,
    As much as the song the Spring.
Aye, many a heart could find content
If it saw the joy on the road it went
    The joy ahead when it had to grieve—
    For the joy is there—but you have to believe.

A FAREWELL

Charles Kingsley
1819-1875

Charles Kingsley, an Episcopal clergy-man in England, is well known as the author of Westward Ho and The Water Babies and the poems Three Fishers and The Sands of Dee. The last four lines of A Farewell poem are much quoted.

My fairest child, I have no song to give you;
   No lark could pipe to skies so dull and gray;
Yet, ere we part, one lesson I can leave you
   For every day.

     *   *   *   *   *

Be good, sweet maid, and let who will be clever;
   Do noble things, not dream them, all day long;
And so make life, death, and that vast forever
   One grand, sweet song.

 # UP-HILL

Christina Rossetti
1830-1894

Christina Rossetti was the daughter of Gabriel Rossetti, professor of Litera-ture in King's college, and sister of Dante Gabriel Rossetti. The father was an enthusiastic student of the Italian poet Dante, and the son a leader in the movement to idealize the emotional life of the Middle Ages. All three were deeply spiritual.

Does the road wind up-hill all the way?
   Yes, to the very end.
Will the day's journey take the whole long day?
   From morn to night, my friend.

But is there for the night a resting place?
   A roof when the slow dark hours begin.
May not the darkness hide it from my face?
   You cannot miss that inn.

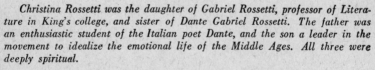

Shall I meet other wayfarers at night?
    Those who have gone before.
Then must I knock, or call when just in sight?
    They will not keep you standing at that door.

Shall I find comfort, travel-sore and weak?
    Of labor you shall find the sum.
Will there be beds for me and all who seek?
    Yea, beds for all who come.

THE GOAL

Ella Wheeler Wilcox

1855-1919

Religion presents few difficulties to the humble; many to the proud; insuperable ones to the vain.—Hare.

All roads that lead to God are good;
    What matters it, your faith or mine;
    Both center at the goal divine
Of love's eternal brotherhood.

A thousand creeds have come and gone;
    But what is that to you or me?
    Creeds are but branches of a tree,
The root of love lives on and on.

Though branch by branch proves withered wood,
    The root is warm with precious wine;
    Then keep your faith, and leave me mine;
All roads that lead to God are good.

IF ONLY THE DREAMS ABIDE

Clinton Scollard

1862-1932

"Our youth and our manhood are due to our country but our declining years are due to ourselves," says Pliny. John Burroughs was Waiting—

> *The stars come nightly to the sky;*
> *The tidal wave unto the sea;*
> *Nor time, nor space, nor deep, nor high,*
> *Can keep my own away from me.*

As we sow, so shall we reap. Scollard would be satisfied if only the dreams abide.

If the things of earth must pass
Like the dews upon the grass,
Like the mists that break and run
At the forward sweep of the sun,
I shall be satisfied
If only the dreams abide.

Nay, I would not be shorn
Of gold from the mines of morn!
I would not be bereft
Of the last blue flower in the cleft,—
Of the blaze that haunts the hills,
Or the moon that midnight fills!
Still would I know the grace
Upon love's uplifted face,
And the slow, sweet joy-dawn there
Under the dusk of her hair.

I pray thee, spare me, Fate,
The woeful, wearying weight
Of a heart that feels no pain
At the sob of the Autumn rain,
And takes no breath of glee
From the organ-surge of the sea,—
Of a mind where memory broods
Over songless solitudes!
I shall be satisfied
If only the dreams abide.

SONNET

"The World Is Too Much
With Us"

William Wordsworth

1770-1850

Beauty seen is partly in him who sees it.—Bovee.

The World is too much with us; late and soon,
Getting and spending, we lay waste our powers;
Little we see in Nature that is ours;
We have given our hearts away, a sordid boon!
This sea that bares her bosom to the moon;
The winds that will be howling at all hours,
And are up-gathered now like sleeping flowers;
For this, for everything, we are out of tune;
It moves us not.—Great God! I'd rather be
A Pagan suckled in a creed outworn,
So might I, standing on this pleasant lea,
Have glimpses that would make me less forlorn;
Have sight of Proteus rising from the sea,
Or hear old Triton blow his wreathed horn.

AWARENESS
Miriam Teichner
1888-

The sensitive soul must sometimes—often—feel incompetent to harvest the beauty that lies about us. And more poignant yet is the fear that age and surfeit shall come, as Tennyson says, "like dull narcotics numbing pain."

Miriam Teichner, poet and newspaper woman, prays: "Let me be aware."

God—let me be aware.
Let me not stumble blindly down the ways,
Just getting somehow safely through the days,
Not even groping for another hand,
Not even wondering why it all was planned,
Eyes to the ground unseeking for the light,
Soul never aching for a wild-winged flight,
Please, keep me eager just to do my share.
God—let me be aware.

God—let me be aware.
Stab my soul fiercely with others' pain,
Let me walk seeing horror and stain.
Let my hands, groping, find other hands.
Give me the heart that divines, understands.
Give me the courage, wounded, to fight.
Flood me with knowledge, drench me in light.
Please—keep me eager just to do my share.
God—let me be aware.

 ## THE FREEMAN'S CREED
Anonymous

Following is the inscription on the statue of the Minuteman at Springfield, New Jersey.

Of what avail the plow or sail
Or land or life, if freedom fail?

GOOD-NIGHT

Nancy Byrd Turner

This gentle poem, though of trite conception, redeems itself through its ingenuous hearth-devotion. The author was sometime editor of the children's page of the Youth's Companion.

"Good-night, sleep well!" we say to those we love,
And watch dear faces glimmer on the stair,
And hear faint footfalls in the rooms above
        Sound on the quiet air,
Yet feel no fear, though lonely they must go
The road of slumber's strange oblivion:
        Dark always wears to dawn,
Sleep is so gentle, and so well we know,
        Wherever they have gone,
They will be safe until the morning light,
        Good-night, good-night!

Good night, sleep well, beloveds, when the last
Slow dusk has fallen, and your steps no more
Make music on the empty upper floor,
        And day is fully past.
We who so lightly let you go alone,
Evening by evening, from our trustful sight
Into the mystery of sleep's unknown—
        We need not fear, tonight,
Death is so gentle—dark will break to dawn....
Love will be safe until the morning light.
        Sleep well, good-night!

BY BENDEMEER'S STREAM

Thomas Moore

1779-1852

Thomas Moore, best loved of Irish poets, is known for the lyric quality of his poems. Many of them have been set to music, including this.

There's a bower of roses by Bendemeer's stream,
    And the nightingale sings round it all the day long;
In the time of my childhood 'twas like a sweet dream,
    To sit in the roses and hear the bird's song.

That bower and its music I never forget,
    But oft when alone, in the bloom of the year,
I think—is the nightingale singing there yet?
    Are the roses still bright by the calm Bendemeer?

No, the roses soon wither'd that hung o'er the wave,
    But some blossoms were gather'd while freshly they shone,
And a dew was distilled from their flowers, that gave
    All the fragrance of summer, when summer was gone.

Thus memory draws from delight, ere it dies,
    An essence that breathes of it many a year;
Thus bright to my soul, as 'twas then to my eyes,
    Is that bower on the banks of the calm Bendemeer!

 BUT ONCE

Anonymous

I expect to pass thru this world but once;
Any good thing, therefore, that I can do,
Or any kindness that I can show to my fellow-creatures,
Let me do it now;
Let me not defer or neglect it,
For I shall not pass this way again.

THE ROUND TRIP
McLandburgh Wilson

This is one of the poems of the Great War. It is a two stanza history of a People.

In swaddling clothes he came across the sea
    In flight from wrong,
Before his eyes all vast blue mystery,
    Waves rolling along,
And in his ears an Old World melody—
    His mother's song.

In khaki he goes back across the sea
    To smite a wrong,
Before his eyes the ocean majesty
    Outraged too long,
And in his ears "My Country, 'Tis of Thee"—
    His mother's song.

THE HUMAN TOUCH
Richard Burton
1859-

High thoughts and noble in all lands
    Help me; my soul is fed by such.
But ah, the touch of lips and hands,—
    The human touch!
Warm, vital, close, life's symbols dear,—
These need I most, and now, and here.

THE SAILOR BOY

Alfred Tennyson

1809-1892

If youth does not understand maturity, it is equally true that maturity has forgotten what it is to be young.

> *Youth is hot and bold, age is weak and cold;*
> *Youth is wild, and age is tame.*
> —*Shakspere, The Passionate Pilgrim.*

He rose at dawn and, fired with hope,
    Shot o'er the seething harbor-bar,
And reach'd the ship and caught the rope,
    And whistled to the morning star.

And while he whistled long and loud
    He heard a fierce mermaiden cry,
"O boy, tho thou art young and proud,
    I see the place where thou wilt lie.

"The sands and yeasty surges mix
    In caves about the dreary bay,
And on thy ribs the limpet sticks,
    And in thy heart the scrawl shall play."

"Fool," he answer'd, "death is sure
    To those that stay and those that roam,
But I will nevermore endure
    To sit with empty hands at home.

"My mother clings about my neck,
    My sisters crying, 'Stay for shame';
My father raves of death and wreck,—
    They are all to blame, they are all to blame.

"God help me! save I take my part
    Of danger on the roaring sea,
A devil rises in my heart,
    Far worse than any death to me."

PICTURES OF MEMORY

Alice Cary

1820-1871

Alice and Phoebe Cary were inseparable sisters, among a family of nine reared in the Miami valley in Ohio. They wrote poetry in spite of the labors of their frontier home, and they sent much of it to publishers where at last their writings came to the attention of Horace Greeley who invited them to New York. There they met Whittier who wrote a poem about Alice. Ultimately they moved to New York where Alice died in 1871, and Phoebe, unable to bear her loneliness, followed in a few months.

Among the beautiful pictures
    That hang on Memory's wall,
Is one of a dim old forest
    That seemeth best of all:
Not for its gnarled oaks olden,
    Dark with the mistletoe;
Not for the violets golden
    That sprinkle the vale below;
Not for the milk-white lilies
    That lean from the fragrant hedge,
Coquetting all day with the sunbeams,
    And stealing their shining edge;
Not for the vines on the upland
    Where the bright red berries be,
Not the pinks, nor the pale sweet cowslip
    It seemeth the best to me.

I once had a little brother
    With eyes that were dark and deep—
In the lap of that old dim forest
    He lieth in peace asleep:
Light as the down of the thistle,
    Free as the winds that blow,
We roved there the beautiful summers,
    The summers of long ago;

But his feet on the hills grew weary,
    And, one of the autumn eves,
I made for my little brother
    A bed of the yellow leaves.

Sweetly his pale arms folded
    My neck in a meek embrace,
As the light of immortal beauty
    Silently covered his face:
And when the arrows of sunset
    Lodged in the tree tops bright,
He fell, in his saint-like beauty,
    Asleep by the gates of light.
Therefore, of all the pictures
    That hang on Memory's wall,
The one of the old dim forest
    Seemeth the best of all.

WHEN THE KYE COMES HAME

James Hogg

1770-1835

The second greatest peasant poet of Scotland, James Hogg, was a good shepherd about his native heaths in youth, but like his confrere Burns, a poor farmer in manhood. He possessed many of the characteristics of Burns, especially his ability to glorify the homely peasant life of his people. Hogg was a friend of Sir Walter Scott and furnished him with several border ballads and much local color.

Come all ye jolly shepherds
    That whistle through the glen,
I'll tell ye of a secret
    That courtiers dinna ken:
What is the greatest bliss
    That the tongue o' man can name?
'T is to woo a bonnie lassie

When the kye comes hame.
When the kye comes hame,
   When the kye comes hame,
'Tween the gloamin' and the mirk,
   When the kye comes hame.

'T is not beneath the coronet,
   Nor canopy of state,
'T is not on couch of velvet,
   Nor arbor of the great:
'T is beneath the spreading birk,
   In the dell without a name,
Wi' a bonnie, bonnie lassie
   When the kye comes hame.

There the blackbird bigs his nest
   For the mate he lo'es to see,
And up upon the tapmost bough,
   O, a happy bird is he!
Then he pours his melting ditty,
   And love 't is a' the theme,
And he'll woo his bonnie lassie
   When the kye comes hame.

When the bluart bears a pearl,
   And the daisy turns a pea,
And the bonnie lucken gowan
   Has fauldit up his e'e,
Then the laverock frae the blue lift
   Doops down, and thinks nae shame
To woo his bonnie lassie
   When the kye comes hame.

Then since all nature joins
   In this love without alloy,
Wha wad prove a traitor
   To Nature's dearest joy?
O, wha wad choose a crown,
   Wi' its perils and its fame,
And miss his bonnie lassie
   When the kye comes hame?

See yonder pawky shepherd
    That lingers on the hill—
His yowes are in the fauld,
    And his lambs are lying still;
Yet he downa gang to rest,
    For his heart is in a flame
To meet his bonnie lassie
    When the kye comes hame.

When the little wee bit heart
    Rises high in the breast,
An' the little wee bit starn
    Rises red in the east,
O, there's a joy so dear
    That the heart can hardly frame,
Wi' a bonnie, bonnie lassie
    When the kye comes hame.

MORALITY

Matthew Arnold
1822-1888

This is but one of the six stanzas written by Arnold in 1852. Man has a true guide to industry if "the tasks of insight willed, can be through the hours of gloom fulfilled," a forward vision if with Gilman (p. 67), he resolve "Never to look behind me for an hour," and motive if after Van Dyke (p. 64), he can say, "My heart shall keep the courage of the quest."

We cannot kindle when we will
The fire which in the heart resides;
The spirit bloweth and is still,
In mystery our soul abides.
    But tasks in hours of insight will'd
    Can be through hours of gloom fulfill'd.

THE PROSE-POETRY
OF LINCOLN

Abraham Lincoln
1809-1865

Few of us realize that part of the beauty of our greatest prose is due to the poetic rhythm of its phrases. Great thoughts are given place and importance and period, and contributing phrases are laid about them—not designedly, but naturally after the poetic instincts of the soul.

The last paragraph of the First Inaugural—

I am loath to close.
We are not enemies, but friends.

We must not be enemies.
    Though passion may have strained,
It must not break our bonds of affection.

The mystic chords of memory,
    Stretching from every battlefield and patriot **grave**
    To every living heart and hearthstone
    All over this broad land,
Will yet swell the chorus of the Union
    When again touched,
    As surely they will be,
By the better angels of our nature.

The closing paragraph of the Second Inaugural—

With malice toward none;
With charity for all;
With firmness in the right,
    As God gives us to see the right,

Let us strive on to finish the work we are in;
To bind up the nation's wounds;
To care for him who shall have borne the battle,
    And for his widow,
    And his orphan—
To do all which may achieve and cherish a just and lasting
   peace
Among ourselves, and with all nations.

WHY?

Anonymous

Leaves have their time to fall, and flowers to wither at the north-wind's breath, and stars to set—but all, thou hast all seasons for thine own, O death!—Mrs. Hemans.

When the veil from the eyes is lifted
    The seer's head is gray;
When the sailor to shore has drifted
    The sirens are far away.
Why should this clearer vision—
    The wisdom of Life's late hour—
Come, as in Fate's derision,
    When the hand has lost its power?

O for the young man's fancies!
    O for the old man's will!
Those flee, while this advances—
    And the strong years cheat us still.

THE MOUNTAIN GIRL

DuBose Heyward

1885-

DuBose Heyward, a descendant of Thomas Savage Heyward, one of the signers of the Declaration of Independence, is the poet of the Carolinas. He knows and loves the simple people of the hills, who in Spring come down to the town—

> *"Leading a spotted heifer, or a steer,*
> *A rangy mule or two, a pair of hounds...*
> *The girls go flocking up and down the street,*
> *A startled wonder in their hill-blue eyes,*
> *.....these people that I know*
> *And understand a little and love much."*
> *—The Mountain Town.*

Life ripens swiftly in these lonely hills,
Ripens, then hangs long-withered on the bough.
Out of their ancient hates, relentless wills,
And unsaid loves, youth burgeons fierce and strong,
Ready for life when life has scarce begun;
Eager to spend its all and then be done.

So, as I gaze at Dorothea now,
Wind-blown against the cabin's weathered side,
Defiant, flushed, with bodice blowing wide,
And rain-soaked homespun skirt that cannot hide
The bold, strong, ardent curves of womanhood;
My exultation winces into pain.

From *Skylines and Horizons* by DuBose Heyward. By permission of the Publishers, Farrar & Rinehart.

Youth, splendid, careless, racing with the rain,
Laughing against the storm as it shouts by.
And yet, perhaps when I pass here again,
Hid from the beat of weathers, she will be
One of the sunken, burned-out lives I see
Here where the mountains shoulder to the sky.

So, as the storm goes smashing down the range,
Striking white fire from the smitten hills,
Swelling the falls and streams until it fills
The cove with giant's music, wild and strange,
The laugh she sends across the shaken air
Brings sudden tears; its very triumph sings
Of beauty so intense it cannot last
Beyond the transient day of fragile things
That brush us, like a wind from unseen wings,
And then are gathered up into the past.

IRONY
Mabel Wing Castle

*Irony is the most vaguely defined word in the language. It is defined some-
times to mean almost what innuendo better expresses, and very commonly as
refined sarcasm. Whatever may be its definition, here is an exact and artistic
illustration of its meaning.*

A dime I gave for sterling
    Came back a counterfeit;
I turned my purse out, testing
    Each coin, so fearing cheat.
My golden eagle? Sternly
    I flung it on a stone,
It slipped from sight forever—
    Ringing the truest tone.

THE DREAMERS
Theodosia Garrison
1874-

He who is not contented with what he has would not be contented with what he would like to have.

The gypsies passed her little gate—
    She stopped her wheel to see—
A brown-faced pair who walked the road,
    Free as the wind is free;
And suddenly her tidy room
    A prison seemed to be.

Her shining plate against the walls,
    Her sunlit, sanded floor,
The brass-bound wedding chest that held
    Her linen's snowy store,
The very wheel whose humming died,—
    Seemed only chains she bore.

She watched the foot-free gypsies pass;
    She never knew or guessed
The wistful dream that drew them close—
    The longing in each breast
Some day to know a home like hers,
    Wherein their hearts might rest.

 ## A THOUGHT TO REMEMBER
Robert Louis Stevenson
1850-1894

There is so much bad in the best of us
And so much good in the worst of us,
That it ill behooves any of us
To talk about the rest of us.

ALADDIN

James Russell Lowell

1819-1891

Only the aged gold of courage can replace the resplendent silvers of youth.

When I was a beggarly boy,
 And lived in a cellar damp,
I had not a friend nor a toy,
 But I had Aladdin's lamp;
When I could not sleep for the cold,
 I had fire enough in my brain,
And builded, with roofs of gold,
 My beautiful castles in Spain!

Since then I have toiled day and night,
 I have money and power good store,
But I'd give all my lamps of silver bright
 For the one that is mine no more.
Take, Fortune, whatever you choose;
 You gave, and may snatch again;
I have nothing 'twould pain me to lose,
 For I own no more castles in Spain!

A SPARK O' NATURE'S FIRE

Robert Burns

1759-1796

Gie me ae spark o' Nature's fire!
That's a' the learning I desire;
Then though I drudge through dub and mire
  At pleugh or cart,
My Muse, though hamely in attire,
  May touch the heart.

THE PATTER OF THE RAIN

Coates Kinney

1826-1904

Among the school book recitations of a generation ago is this gem of metre and memory. A poem of our less critical years, it yet wears well. Coates Kinney has long been dead, and the poetry he represented is for the most part dead —more jingle than metre and more implied majesty than spiritual intuition. But the little poem will live long.

When the humid shadows hover
 Over all the starry spheres,
And the melancholy darkness
 Gently weeps in raining tears,
What a joy to press the pillow
 Of a cottage chamber bed,
And to listen to the patter
 Of the soft rain overhead.

Every patter on the shingles
 Has an echo of the heart,
Many long-forgotten fancies
 Into being quickly start,
And a thousand recollections
 Weave their bright hues into **woof,**
As I listen to the patter
 Of the soft rain on the roof.

Now in memory comes my mother,
 As she used long years agone,
To regard the darling dreamers,
 Ere she left them to the dawn.
Oh! I see her bending o'er me
 As I list to the refrain
Which is played upon the shingles
 By the patter of the rain.

INTIMATIONS OF IMMORTALITY

William Wordsworth

1770-1850

Wordsworth says of his childhood that he could never "admit the notion of death as a state applicable to my own being." He felt that life was but a wayside diversion from Eternity. Only parts of the first and the fifth stanzas are given.

There was a time when meadow, grove, and stream,
The earth, and every common sight
  To me did seem
  Apparell'd in celestial light,
The glory and the freshness of a dream.

  * * * * *

Our birth is but a sleep and a forgetting,
The Soul that rises with us, our life's Star,
  Hath had elsewhere its setting
  And cometh from afar;
  Not in entire forgetfulness,
  And not in utter nakedness,
But trailing clouds of glory we do come
  From God, who is our home:
Heaven lies about us in our infancy!
Shades of the prison-house begin to close
  Upon the growing Boy,
But he beholds the light, and whence it flows,
  He sees it in his joy;
The Youth, who daily farther from the east
  Must travel, still is Nature's priest,
  And by the vision splendid
  Is on his way attended;
At length the Man perceives it die away,
And fade into the light of common day.

INDEX

PAGE

A Ballad of Heroes—*Austin Dobson*...................... 114
A Farewell—*Charles Kingsley* 128
A Fear—*Ruth Messenger* 97
A Hero—*Florence Earle Coates*......................... 53
A Little Prayer—*Samuel Ellsworth Kiser*.................. 80
A Little While I Fain Would Linger Yet—*Paul Hamilton*
    Hayne 29
A Noiseless, Patient Spider—*Walt Whitman*............... 36
A Rhyme for Thanksgiving—*Edwin Markham*.............. 112
A Song of Life—*Angela Morgan*......................... 108
A Spark o' Nature's Fire—*Robert Burns*.................. 146
A Thought to Remember—*Robert Louis Stevenson*.......... 145
Akins, Zoë—One Woman................................. 47
Alderson, Alethea Todd—In a Public Library.............. 117
Aladdin—*James Russell Lowell*.......................... 146
Allingham, William—Solitude 95
America the Beautiful—*Katherine Lee Bates*............... 98
Anonymous—But Once 134
    Death I Can Understand........................... 71
    I Am the Door.................................... 72
    I Teach School 16
    My Daily Creed................................... 94
    Myself 45
    Playing the Game................................. 110
    Sin Is Sin.. 86
    The Freeman's Creed.............................. 132
    Why? 142
Arnold, Matthew—Morality 140
    Self-Dependence 18
As in Silks My Julia Goes—*Robert Herrick*................ 22
As Toilsome I Wandered—*Walt Whitman*.................. 20
At the Crossroads—*Richard Hovey*....................... 88
Auld Daddy Darkness—*James Ferguson*................... 65

[149]

PAGE

Awareness—*Miriam Teichner* 132
Barnett, Mavis Clare—Silence........................... 48
Bates, Katherine Lee—America the Beautiful.............. 98
Beeman, Katherine—Happiness 100
Bendemeer's Stream—*Thomas Moore*..................... 134
Bible—I Will Lift Up Mine Eyes........................ 86
    Remember Now 37
Bierce, Ambrose—Creation 25
Borrowing Trouble—*Robert Burns*....................... 36
Browning, Elizabeth Barrett—Cares 19
Browning, Robert—Prospice 43
Bruce to His Men—*Robert Burns*........................ 40
Bryant, William Cullen—So Live........................ 31
Building the Bridge for Him—*W. A. Dromgoole*........... 13
Burnet, Dana—The Homeland 110
Burns, Robert—A Spark o' Nature's Fire.................. 146
    Borrowing Trouble 36
    Bruce to His Men.................................. 40
    Epistle to a Young Friend.......................... 49
    From His First Song............................... 91
Burton, Richard—The Human Touch..................... 135
    But Once 134
By an Open Window in Church—*Corinne Roosevelt Robinson*. 23
Byron—*Joaquin Miller* 38
Byron, Lord—Sonnet on Chillon........................ 77
Called Back—*Emily Dickinson*.......................... 75
Cares—*Elizabeth Barrett Browning*...................... 19
Carman, Bliss—Over the Shoulders and Slopes of the Dune... 14
Cary, Alice—Pictures of Memory........................ 137
Cary, Phoebe—Nearer Home............................ 101
Castle, Mabel Wing—Irony............................. 144
Clough, Arthur Hugh—Say Not the Struggle Nought Availeth. 28
Coates, Florence Earle—A Hero......................... 53
    Per Aspera 100
Colton, Buel P.—Keep Thou My Heart................... 17
Company—*Richard R. Kirk*............................. 74
Coolidge, Susan—New Every Morning.................... 76

PAGE

Courage—*Amelia Earhart* 102

Cowards—*William Shakspere* 72

Creation—*Ambrose Bierce* 25

Death I Can Understand—*Anonymous* 71

Delight in Disorder—*Robert Herrick* 22

Dickinson, Emily—Called Back 75

Dobson, Austin—A Ballad of Heroes 114

    The Rose and the Gardener 85

Dromgoole, W. A.—Building the Bridge for Him 13

Dudley, Bide—To James Whitcomb Riley 62

Dusk—*Clinton Scollard* 105

Earhart, Amelia—Courage 102

En Garde, Messieurs—*William Lindsay* 73

Epistle to a Young Friend—*Robert Burns* 49

Ferguson, James—Auld Daddy Darkness 65

Field, Eugene—The Wanderer 52

Flower in the Crannied Wall—*Alfred Tennyson* 21

Fortune's Finger—*William Shakspere* 14

Fowler, Ellen Thornycroft—The Wisdom of Folly 87

From His First Song—*Robert Burns* 91

From the Arabian—Three Gates 99

"Frost Tonight"—*Edith M. Thomas* 25

Gale, Norman—The Second Coming 48

Garrison, Theodosia—One Fight More 70

    The Dreamers 145

Gates—Ellen E. M.—The Bars of Fate 66

German Prisoners—*Joseph Johnston Lee* 42

Gilman, Charlotte Perkins—I Resolve 67

    The Lion Path 116

Good-By—To My Mother—*Margaret Larkin* 41

Good Deeds—*William Shakspere* 120

Good Night—*Nancy Byrd Turner* 133

Gradatim—*J. G. Holland* 79

Happiness—*Katherine Beeman* 100

Hayne, Paul Hamilton—A Little While I Fain Would

    Linger Yet 29

He Whom a Dream Hath Possessed—*Sheamus O'Sheel* 126

PAGE

He's Just—Away—*James Whitcomb Riley* 30

Henley, *William Ernest*—So Be My Passing 82

Herbert, *Alice*—Lullaby 27

Herrick, *Robert*—As in Silks My Julia Goes 22

    Delight in Disorder 22

Heyward, *DuBose*—The Mountain Girl 143

Higginson, *Thomas Wentworth*—The Trumpeter 107

Hogg, *James*—When the Kye Comes Hame 138

Holland, *J. G.*—Gradatim 79

Holmes, *Oliver Wendell*—The Boys 33

Home—*Hermann Ford Martin* 44

Hovey, *Richard*—At the Crossroads 88

I Am the Door—*Anonymous* 72

I Fear No Power—*Ernest McGaffey* 95

I Resolve—*Charlotte Perkins Gilman* 67

I Shall Not Make a Garment of My Grief—*Roselle Mercier*

    Montgomery 109

I Teach School—*Anonymous* 16

I Will Lift Up Mine Eyes—*Bible* 86

If Only the Dreams Abide—*Clinton Scollard* 130

If Still They Live—*Edith M. Thomas* 58

If This Were Faith—*Robert Louis Stevenson* 84

Immortal Craftsmen—*Daniel Webster* 71

In a Public Library—*Alethea Todd Alderson* 117

Inscription—*Sir William Watson* 42

Interlude—*Ella Wheeler Wilcox* 111

Intimations of Immortality—*William Wordsworth* 148

Irony—*Mabel Wing Castle* 144

It May Be—*Samuel Ellsworth Kiser* 96

Jackson, *Helen Hunt*—Spinning 32

Janis, *Elsie*—My Prayer 120

Jones, *Thomas S., Jr.*—Sometimes 125

Keep Thou My Heart—*Buel P. Colton* 17

Kingsley, *Charles*—A Farewell 128

    The Sands of Dee 90

Kinney, *Coates*—The Patter of the Rain 147

Kipling, *Rudyard*—The Bell Buoy 92

PAGE

Kirk, Richard R.—Company............................ 78
Kiser, Samuel Ellsworth—A Little Prayer.................. 80
    It May Be... 96
Landor, Walter Savage—Plays............................ 74
Lang, Andrew—Scythe Song.............................. 91
Larkin, Margaret—Good-By—To My Mother............... 41
Lee, Joseph Johnston—German Prisoners.................... 42
Leland, Charles Godfrey—The Two Friends................. 63
Let Me Live Out My Years—*John G. Neihardt*.............. 35
Letts, Winifred M.—The Spires of Oxford.................. 54
Life—*Edward Rowland Sill*.............................. 105
Light Within—*John Milton*.............................. 17
Lincoln, Abraham—The Prose-Poetry of Lincoln........... 141
Lindsay, William—En Garde, Messieurs.................... 73
Litchfield, Grace Denio—To a Hurt Child.................. 81
Longfellow, Henry Wadsworth—Nature.................... 124
    The Old Clock on the Stairs.......................... 68
Love Slumbers On—*Percy Bysshe Shelley*.................. 125
Lowell, James Russell—Aladdin.......................... 146
Lullaby—*Alice Herbert* 27
Mackay, Charles—No Enemies............................ 21
Malloch, Douglas—You Have to Believe................... 127
Malone, Walter—Opportunity 55
Markham, Edwin—A Rhyme for Thanksgiving............. 112
Martin, Hermann Ford—Home........................... 44
McGaffey, Ernest—I Fear No Power...................... 95
Messenger, Ruth—A Fear............................... 97
Miller, Cincinnatus Hiner (Joaquin)—Byron.............. 38
Milton, John—Light Within............................. 17
    Sonnet on His Blindness.............................. 26
Montgomery, Roselle Mercier—I Shall Not Make a Gar-
    ment of My Grief.................................... 109
Moore, Thomas—Bendemeer's Stream.................... 134
Morality—*Matthew Arnold* 140
Morgan, Angela—A Song of Life......................... 108
Mors Benefica—*Edmund Clarence Stedman*................ 115
My Creed—*Howard Arnold Walter*....................... 26

PAGE

My Daily Creed—*Anonymous*........................... 94

My Prayer—*Elsie Janis* 120

My Task—*Robert Louis Stevenson*....................... 39

My Wage—*Jessie B. Rittenhouse*........................ 123

Myself—*Anonymous* 45

Nature—*Henry Wadsworth Longfellow*.................... 124

Nearer Home—*Phoebe Cary*............................. 101

Neihardt, John G.—Let Me Live Out My Years............. 35

New Every Morning—*Susan Coolidge*.................... 76

No Enemies—*Charles Mackay*........................... 21

Nostalgia—*Elizabeth Virginia Raplee*................... 24

One Fight More—*Theodosia Garrison*.................... 70

One Woman—*Zoë Akins* 47

Opportunity—*Walter Malone* 55

O'Sheel, Sheamus—He Whom a Dream Hath Possessed...... 126

Over the Shoulders and Slopes of the Dune—*Bliss Carman*.... 14

Ozymandias of Egypt—*Percy Bysshe Shelley*.............. 83

Per Aspera—*Florence Earle Coates*...................... 100

Pictures of Memory—*Alice Cary*........................ 137

Playing the Game—*Anonymous*......................... 110

Plays—*Walter Savage Landor*........................... 74

Poise—*Viola Alleyn Storey*............................. 27

Pope, Alexander—Vice 35

    Words 83

Proctor, Edna Dean—Take Heart........................ 15

Prospice—*Robert Browning* 43

Raplee, Elizabeth Virginia—Nostalgia................... 24

Read, Thomas Buchanan—The Brave at Home............. 46

Reese, Lizette Woodworth—Tears........................ 56

Remember Now—*Bible* 37

Rice, Cale Young—The Mystic........................... 60

Riley, James Whitcomb—He's Just—Away................. 30

    The Parting Guest................................. 62

Rittenhouse, Jessie B.—My Wage........................ 123

    The Ghostly Galley................................ 107

Robinson, Corinne Roosevelt—By an Open Window in Church 23

Rorty, James—The Bell................................. 103

PAGE

Rossetti, Christina—Up Hill.............................. 128
Say Not the Struggle Nought Availeth—*Arthur Hugh Clough*.. 28
Scollard, Clinton—Dusk 105
     If Only the Dreams Abide.......................... 130
     The Great Voice.................................. 96
Self-Dependence—*Matthew Arnold* 18
Shakspere, William—Cowards 72
     Fortune's Finger 14
     Good Deeds 120
     Thrice Armed 81
     Tomorrow and Tomorrow.......................... 74
     Uneasy Lies the Head............................ 57
     Why Should a Man................................ 45
Shelley, Percy Bysshe—Love Slumbers On................ 125
     Ozymandias of Egypt............................. 83
Silence—*Mavis Clare Barnett*............................ 48
Sill, Edward Rowland—Life.............................. 105
Sin Is Sin—*Anonymous*.................................. 86
So Be My Passing—*William Ernest Henley*................ 82
So Live—*William Cullen Bryant*.......................... 31
Solitude—*William Allingham* 95
Sometimes—*Thomas S. Jones, Jr*......................... 125
Sonnet—*William Wordsworth* 131
Sonnet on Chillon—*Lord Byron* 77
Sonnet on His Blindness—*John Milton*.................... 26
Spinning—*Helen Hunt Jackson*........................... 32
Standards—*Charles Wharton Stork*....................... 89
Starbuck, Victor—The Dead.............................. 78
Stedman, Edmund Clarence—Mors Benefica................ 115
Stevenson, Robert Louis—A Thought to Remember.......... 145
     If This Were Faith............................... 84
     My Task 39
     Windy Nights 113
Storey, Viola Alleyn—Poise............................. 27
Stork, Charles Wharton—Standards...................... 89
Scythe Song—*Andrew Lang*............................... 91
Take Heart—*Edna Dean Proctor*.......................... 15

PAGE

Tears—*Lizette Woodworth Reese* 56
Teichner, Miriam—Awareness 132
    The Struggle 123
    Victory 39
Tennyson, Alfred—Flower in the Crannied Wall............ 21
    The Greatness of the Soul........................... 104
    The Sailor Boy..................................... 136
    Ulyssus 106
The Bars of Fate—*Ellen E. M. Gates*..................... 66
The Bell—*James Rorty* 103
The Bell Buoy—*Rudyard Kipling*...................... 92
The Boys—*Olivr Wendell Holmes*...................... 33
The Brave at Home—*Thomas Buchanan Read*............... 46
The Dead—*Victor Starbuck* 78
The Dreamers—*Theodosia Garrison* 145
The Eternal Goodness—*John Greenleaf Whittier*............ 118
The Freeman's Creed—*Anonymous* 132
The Ghostly Galley—*Jessie B. Rittenhouse*................ 107
The Goal—*Ella Wheeler Wilcox*.......................... 129
The Great Voice—*Clinton Scollard*....................... 96
The Greatness of the Soul—*Alfred Tennyson*............... 104
The Homeland—*Dana Burnet* 110
The Human Touch—*Richard Burton*...................... 135
The Last Tourney—*Frederic F. Van de Water*............. 59
The Lion Path—*Charlotte Perkins Gilman*................. 116
The Mountain Girl—*DuBose Heyward*..................... 143
The Mystic—*Cale Young Rice*............................ 60
The Old Clock on the Stairs—*Henry Wadsworth Longfellow*.. 68
The Patter of the Rain—*Coates Kinney*................... 147
The Parting Guest—*James Whitcomb Riley*................ 62
The Prose-Poetry of Lincoln—*Abraham Lincoln*............ 141
The Rose and the Gardener—*Austin Dobson*................ 85
The Round Trip—*McLandburgh Wilson*................... 135
The Sailor Boy—*Alfred Tennyson*........................ 136
The Sands of Dee—*Charles Kingsley*...................... 90
The Second Coming—*Norman Gale*....................... 48
The Spires of Oxford—*Winifred M. Letts*................. 54

PAGE

The Struggle—*Miriam Teichner* 123

The Trailing Arbutus—*John Greenleaf Whittier* 122

The Trumpeter—*Thomas Wentworth Higginson* 107

The Two Friends—*Charles Godfrey Leland* 63

The Wanderer—*Eugene Field* 52

The Wisdom of Folly—*Ellen Thornycroft Fowler* 87

The World Is Too Much with Us—*William Wordsworth* 131

The World's Needs—*Ella Wheeler Wilcox* 53

The Zest of Life—*Henry van Dyke* 64

They Sleep So Quietly—*Virginia Lyne Tunstall* 121

Thomas, Edith M.—"Frost Tonight" 25

    If Still They Live 58

Three Gates—*From the Arabian* 99

Thrice Armed—*William Shakspere* 81

To a Hurt Child—*Grace Denio Litchfield* 81

To James Whitcomb Riley—*Bide Dudley* 62

Tomorrow and Tomorrow—*William Shakspere* 74

Tunstall, Virginia Lyne—They Sleep So Quietly 121

Turner, Nancy Byrd—Good Night 133

Ulyssus—*Alfred Tennyson* 106

Uneasy Lies the Head—*William Shakspere* 57

Up Hill—*Christina Rossetti* 128

Van de Water, Frederic F.—The Last Tourney 59

Van *Dyke, Henry*—The Zest of Life 64

Vice—*Alexander Pope* 35

Victory—*Miriam Teichner* 39

Walter, Howard Arnold—My Creed 26

Watson, Sir William—Inscription 42

Webster, Daniel—Immortal Craftsmen 71

When the Kye Comes Hame—*James Hogg* 138

Whitman, Walt—A Noiseless, Patient Spider 36

    As Toilsome I Wandered 20

Whittier, John Greenleaf—The Eternal Goodness 118

    The Trailing Arbutus 122

Why?—*Anonymous* 142

Why Should a Man—*William Shakspere* 45

PAGE

Wilcox, Ella Wheeler—The Goal.......................... 129

    Interlude 111

    The World's Needs................................. 53

Wilson, McLandburgh—The Round Trip.................. 135

Windy Nights—*Robert Louis Stevenson*................... 113

Words—*Alexander Pope* 83

Wordsworth, William—From Intimations of Immortality..... 148

    The World Is Too Much with Us..................... 131

You Have to Believe—*Douglas Malloch*.................. 127